COLORS OF TRUST

Shirley B. Bard

Published by RSE Publishing
403 N. Harper Street, Laurens, SC 29360, U.S.A.

ISBN 978-0-983-71032-5

Printed in the United States of America
Edited by Amanda L. Capps
Cover Art and Design by Dan Fowler
Art for Chapters 14, 15, 17, 26 and "The Rose" by Anna Montanucci
Book Design by Michael Seymour

PUBLISHER'S NOTE

MY GRATITUDE

To the Lord
whose faithfulness made all this possible.

To my late husband, Norval Bard, Sr.
whose constant encouragement was invaluable.

To my son, Dr. Norval Bard, Jr. who spent innumerable
hours dragging me into 21st century computer use.

To Shannon B. Cook and Heather B. Schirduan
(my daughters),
Amanda Capps (editor/media consultant/writer),
friends, and medical doctors, whose caring is priceless.

TABLE OF CONTENTS

INTRODUCTION

Color dominates and captivates. Colors intrude into our emotions and minds with understood and applied meanings. Tradition, gender, and age determine preferences and reactions. Color defines our culture, enriches our vocabulary, and enhances our lives.

Our Lord created color, then purposely gave us eyesight to behold it. He colors the sky, land, and sea without limit or restraint, bringing pleasure to our beauty-hungry souls. Parading through each season and climate, nature marches to the drummer of color in continual cadence. Colors appear everywhere, either in scattered assortments or orderly arrangements. The starkness of winter turns into the pastel abundance of spring that gives way to the lavish hues of summer. The panoramic scene of fall flowers and trees against the intensely blue October sky with dazzling white clouds is as breathtaking as the rainbow's preset hues arched across a stormy backdrop.

The rainbow was God's idea, a gift, a virtual feast for the soul. It was first mentioned in the scriptures after the flood when God chose it to symbolize His promise:

> I set My rainbow in the cloud, and it shall be for the sign of the covenant between Me and the earth.
>
> It shall be, when I bring a cloud over the earth, that the rainbow shall be seen in the cloud;
>
> And I will remember My covenant which is between Me and you and every living creature of all flesh; the waters shall never again become a flood to destroy all flesh.[1]

The Lord has kept His promise down through the ages. We are now the recipients of that promise, reminded of His faithfulness as we (and He) behold the ethereal beauty of His bow in the clouds. His faithfulness touches our cocooned faith to move us toward butterfly trust, to help us endure the changes that lead to maturity. This growing is a God-designed, unique, individual process.

My own faith has been inching its way through years of life-changing experiences toward the security of trust. Since my walk with the Lord is the one I am most familiar with, I shall use my growing pains to illustrate this transformation. These stories tell of times in my life when the Lord chose to respond in unusual ways. To some these stories may seem preposterous. Yet at the time they seemed perfectly normal to me, and satisfied my seeking heart.

Through an experience with the Lord in 1981, I have come to believe that the rainbow, in addition to being the designated sign of His promise to the earth, is pregnant with many promises of God. The seven basic rainbow colors correspond to my first seven chapters, that deal with the basic events in my life, during which I learned the basic promises and truths of the Lord. The rest of the chapters use the colors of an enlarged rainbow to tell of my experiences in learning to trust.

In Hebrew the word "trust" literally means "to be face down, to lie helpless before God." Because the Lord has continued to use the rainbow to convey His truths to me personally, I invite you to span my colors of trust in ever arching upward toward maturity in Him.

SCRIPTURES AND NOTES

1 Genesis 9:13-15

BASIC

RAINBOW

COLORS

Red
The Color of Love

Red excites, pulsates, dominates. Red defines the curve of the rainbow as the longest wavelength, and possibly the widest range of active emotions. Red in flags represents bloodshed by the courageous, whereas red ink signifies debt or error. Red lights at intersections and railroad crossings alert us to danger, whereas red exit signs reassure us.

Red also expresses love the deepest need of us all. Love serves as both track and train; as track by determining the path of our response, and as a train by bringing us to a place of response. Love is visible on Valentine's Day in reds, but less obvious in times of necessary correction or constructive criticism. Love winds through literature, history, and religion interfaced with red. The love of God the Father was revealed through the shed blood of His Son, Jesus Christ, inciting us to believe and receive His perfect love. The apostle John stated unequivocally that "God is Love."[2] He used the Greek word "agape" for love, meaning the selfless love that gives and gives, regardless of the response.

My parents knew this God-kind of love, and dedicated me to the Lord at 14 months. They also knew about human love, for it had prevailed in my mother's decision to say "No" to teaching and "Yes" to my father. Mother had grown up planning to teach, but only single women, men, and husbands were hired in the Great Depression days. Sacrificing her dream of teaching, she and my father married in 1931 in the living room of a parsonage with a single wedding band ceremony. Ten months and two days later I arrived as an expression of my parents' love, and the first grandchild in our family.

I was named "Shirley" by my mother from the heroine in a book, and "Bernice" because my dad insisted I have mother's middle name. Shirley's literal meaning is "a bright, shining meadow" and Bernice, "a forerunner of victory." The spiritual meanings of my names point toward my becoming "restful and peaceful" plus "victorious."

Parents cannot explain why they choose or reject a certain name for a child, so evidently capturing human bent by name is not up to them. God said, "I have called you by your name,"[3] and "Whatever one is, he has been named already."[4] The Lord said to Jeremiah: "Before I formed you in the womb I knew you."[5] Is it not feasible, indeed probable, that God, having given us our unique abilities and possibilities, also names us? Our loving Lord has been in the naming business from the beginning, for He named the stars,[6] Isaac,[7] John the Baptist,[8] and Jesus,[9] to mention just a few. The Lord's names reveal His own literal and spiritual character. Ours do the same. Our names express both who we are and who we are becoming.

Childhood diseases became my nemesis, much to my parents' distress. For instance, at 19 months I caught whooping cough. At 28 months I came down with diphtheria and pneumonia, requiring an emergency tracheostomy. My mother stayed in the hospital room with me the whole ten days and nights, keeping my inner throat tube cleaned out with pipe cleaners. My dad labored longer hours to cover medical expenses and medicines. After the crisis, the trach was removed leaving an inner scar on my trachea plus a visible one at my throat. The bones and muscles in my neck, chest, and back suffered irreparable damage.

I now spoke in the alto range and often had sore throats. I caught measles at the age of five, requiring a second emergency tracheostomy. I can remember trying to breathe as I rode that star-lit night in a speeding, siren-blasting ambulance to the hospital. When the crisis passed, I overheard my doctor say I might never talk again. A short time later as I was coloring pictures with other recovering children in the hospital, they asked, "Can't you say anything?" I decided to find out, for I had to know if my voice was gone or if the trach was the problem. Unaware of any danger, I took out my complete trach and spoke just one word, "Mama," to them. The alarmed medical staff immediately rushed me to OR and reinserted the trach before my throat could swell. These caring ones reprimanded me severely, but the ordeal was worth it because I knew I could still speak.

I never felt as if I fit in with my classmates due to hard breathing, hoarseness, and throat infections. Nevertheless I enjoyed elementary school for I was endowed with a love for learning.

Love has defined the curve of my life as the longest wavelength. It is a distinct entity of many facets and is never static. Love flows up, down, in, and out giving life to my spirit and soul the way my heart pumps "red" life to my body. Several years ago after asking the Lord if there was a difference between divine and human love, He spoke these words deep inside of me:

> I AM LOVE, that is My inherent nature; therefore love flows like a river from Me through all my creation, and returns to Me to be recycled, refreshed, and restored.
>
> Love is not a solid entity, but is a vibrant, moving, ever-changing, force for good. I gave mankind the ability to receive and express this powerful feeling with your emotions, and your will. It makes no difference whether it is love for Me, family, friends, country, nature or the arts, My love imprint stands forever.

We are all endowed with the capacity and the necessity to love and be loved. Of faith, hope, and love, St. Paul said love is the greatest.[10] It inspires humans to survive crises, separations, successes, and sorrows. Love glows incandescently red, shining through the dreams and disasters of us all.

SCRIPTURES and NOTES

2 1 John 4:8
He who does not love does not know God, for God is love.

3 Isaiah 45:3
I will give you the treasures of darkness and hidden riches of secret places, that you may know that I, the Lord, who call you by your name, am the God of Israel.

4 Ecclesiastes 6:10
Whatever one is, he has been named already...; and cannot contend with Him who is mightier than he.

5 Jeremiah 1:5
Before I formed you in the womb I knew you; before you were born I sanctified you.

6 Psalm 147:4
He counts the number of the stars; He called them all by name.

7 Genesis 17:19
Then God said: "No, Sarah your wife shall bear you a son, and you shall call his name Isaac."

8 Luke 1:13
But the angel said to him, "Do not be afraid, Zacharias, for your prayer is heard; and your wife Elizabeth will bear you a son, and you shall call his name John."

9 Luke 1:31
And behold, you will conceive in your womb and bring forth a Son, and shall call His name Jesus.

10 1 Corinthians 13:13
And now abide faith, hope, love, these three; but the greatest of these is love.

ORANGE
The Color of Forgiveness

Moving across the rainbow from red to yellow, we find orange, the warmest and most persuasive of the earth tones. It is a secondary color, depending on red and yellow for its existence, the same way forgiveness is dependent on love and light for its existence. Because we are all imperfect,[11] we need to receive and offer forgiveness.

During childhood, I was aware that my behavior was not always acceptable, requiring the tough love of parental discipline. They taught me the necessity of saying "I am sorry" and the importance of a forgiving spirit to my well-being. This prepared me for the time when I would desire the Lord's forgiveness, the most important of all.

Because my parents had become believers in their early teens, one of the first things they did after marriage was to join a neighborhood Southern Baptist church. However, spiritual matters moved to a back burner for the next four years as they coped with surviving the depression and the needs of a growing family.

Then in 1935 Rev. Olin Gage, a Southern Baptist Seminary student there in Louisville, Kentucky held an old-fashioned tent meeting at the Parkway Ballpark Field located on Eastern Parkway. Large crowds of people gathered nightly to worship under the big tent. They sat on backless pews, and rested their feet on the sawdust-covered ground. Singing the old hymns without accompaniment, they cooled themselves with handheld cardboard fans provided by the local funeral homes. When Mother and I had to go 30 miles away to care for my sick grandmother that summer, Daddy invited Rev. Gage to stay in our home. As they studied the scriptures together, Daddy read the Bible seriously for first time. From then on, Daddy had a love affair with the Bible, reading and studying it daily. Mother joined him in this pursuit of learning, trusting, and praying. Motivated by their love of the Lord Jesus Christ, they taught us four children about trusting Him. A Christian heritage is a gift from the Lord.

My first unusual experience with the Lord occurred at the age of nine when God showed me what heaven must be like. I have heard it said that visions need no interpretation, but dreams do, according to the scriptures. What I experienced must have been a vision as I slept. I saw beyond the midnight-blue sky filled with stars into a rectangular window of heaven, overhead, opened halfway up from the bottom. Ethereal yellow-white light glowed within as if it were noon there. The music flooding the night was harmonious, lilting, and compelling, beautiful beyond anything I had ever heard.

I immediately got out of bed in the dark and went to where my parents were sleeping. Awakening them, I told them I wanted to become a Christian because I had just seen into heaven, and did not want to miss it. They said that I could tell the Lord right then that I believed in Him and I trusted Him to take care of me. And we would talk more about it in the morning.

The next day when I described what I had seen, I told my parents I was now a believer, too.[12] In an appointment with our Pastor, Rev. Lloyd W. Benedict, my parents and he agreed as we talked that I knew what sin was, and that I had indeed asked for and received the Lord's forgiveness. However, my parents asked me to wait a year before becoming a church member. I think they wanted to be sure that I was not joining just because my friends were. When I was 10, I went forward for membership in Third Avenue Baptist Church. I was baptized the following Sunday morning with my best friend, Sherrill Thompson, whose dad also had to work on Sunday nights.

I remember thinking as I went home with my family after being baptized that my soul was without sin at that moment. Many years later I realized this was not a once-in-a-lifetime cleanness, but I could receive the gift of forgiveness daily. Jesus Christ had died for not only for my sinful nature, but also for all the sins I would ever commit, providing me a clean slate every day just for the asking.

I have often wondered, "Why a window of heaven?" Perhaps I had heard that rain came from the windows of heaven in Noah's day,[13] or that blessings could pour through the windows of heaven.[14] I do know that this glimpse into heaven changed my life forever.

Yes, a Christian heritage is a blessing, but it is not enough.

Forgiveness frees us to become the person God intended when He created us. St. Paul wrote, "Be kind to one another, tenderhearted, forgiving one another, even as God in Christ forgave you."[15] King David called the Lord "Jehovah-Nasa," the One-Who-Forgives.[16]

By accepting the Lord's forgiveness, I began to grow from having been only "a loved one" to becoming "a loving one." As sure as orange follows red in the rainbow, so forgiveness follows love in the Lord's plan of promoting trust.

SCRIPTURES and NOTES

11 Romans 3:23

For all have sinned and fall short of the glory of God.

12 Romans 10:9-10

That if you confess with your mouth the Lord Jesus and believe in your heart that God has raised Him from the dead, you will be saved.

For with the heart one believes unto righteousness, and with the mouth confession is made unto salvation.

13 Genesis 7:11

In the six hundredth year of Noah's life, in the second month, the seventeenth day of the month, on that day all the fountains of the great deep were broken up, and the windows of heaven were opened.

14 Malachi 3:10

Bring all the tithes into the storehouse, that there may be food in My house, and try Me now in this, says the Lord of hosts, If I will not open for you the windows of heaven and pour out for you such blessing that there will not be room enough to receive it.

15 Ephesians 4:32

16 Psalm 99:8

You answered them, O Lord our God; You were to them Jehovah-Nasa (God-Who-Forgives,) though You took vengeance on their deeds.

FIRST VIEW INTO HEAVEN

My first unusual experience with the Lord occurred at the age of nine. I saw beyond the midnight-blue sky filled with stars into a rectangular window of heaven, overhead, opened halfway up from the bottom. Ethereal yellow-white light glowed within. The music flooding the night was harmonious, lilting, and compelling, beautiful beyond anything I had ever heard on earth.

I immediately got out of bed in the dark, woke my parents, and told them I wanted to become a Christian, because I had just seen into heaven, and did not want to miss it. They said to tell the Lord right then that I believed in Him and that I trusted Him to take care of me. I am convinced the Lord knew I needed this reality of heaven for assurance and endurance.

YELLOW
The Color of Light

Yellow glows with warmth and light, a perfect symbol of the Lord's radiant light. On the first day of creation, God said, "Let there be light."[17] On the fourth day He made the sun, moon, and stars to give light on the earth,[18] and 4000 years later, Christ came saying, "I am the light of the world."[19] The Psalmist declares, "The Lord covers Himself with light,"[20] as evidenced in His birth, glory, and holiness; He is called the Morning Star,[21] and the true Light.[22]

Stepping into the bright light of new life in Christ both impelled me to please Him and constrained me from selfish and evil pursuits. Walking in the sunlight of getting to know Him, I discovered new thoughts, and desires, one of which was to play the piano. At every church service my longing increased as I watched and heard the musicians. At school, I wondered how my teachers knew what keys to hit when.

When Mother and I went shopping downtown, the only music we heard in a department store in those days came from a musician playing a black grand piano near the back. This talented pianist performed the current popular tunes, seasonal songs, light classical pieces, and bystanders' requests. So fascinated was I with the impromptu chords, arpeggios, and creativity that Mother would let me stay, watch and listen while she shopped in that store.

When I was in the fifth grade my parents bought a used upright piano for $100.00 that they paid off in monthly increments of $5.00. My first teacher was Miss Laura Mae Brown who was also first violinist for the Louisville Philharmonic Orchestra. She taught music in her second floor apartment near Second and Ormsby Streets. I rode a streetcar (and later a bus) to and from my lessons. I learned not only piano basics with scales and pieces, but eventually music theory, hymns, and harmony playing with octaves and chords. I would go early to lessons so I could hand-copy pop music and chord progressions. I loved going to piano lessons because I was inspired by the music and encouraged by my teacher to keep trying.

The early longing I felt at church to learn piano crystallized into a desire to serve the Lord through music. In a couple of years I was playing simple songs for children, then hymns for small assemblies, Vacation Bible Schools, and missions. Eventually I was playing for worship services. Since singing was difficult for me, I found expression through playing the piano and later, the organ. I minored in music at college, and through the years taught music to others. What a blessing and a joy to worship and serve through music!

When I began reading, I devoured Bible stories, fiction, biographies, and the newspaper funnies – everything but mysteries and ghost stories. (They gave me nightmares, . . . and still do.) Bible reading was sporadic during my early teen years. I can remember as I would pass by the living room trying to get ready to go somewhere, Daddy would say, "Shirley – come hear this. It is so good." So I would have to stop and sit down while he read verses from the Bible that he had just come across once again. If there had been any other way from the kitchen to the upstairs other than going past the living room I would have taken it! Nevertheless, by Daddy reading the scriptures aloud, he transmitted to me his love of the Bible and his enjoyment in it.

My favorite uncle, James Moore, was a handsome man with black, wavy hair and deep, clear blue, twinkling eyes. When he was about 30 years old, he left to serve in the Navy during World War II. On his way to Great Lakes, Illinois, he came by our house to say goodbye. Before he left, I handed him a white and orchid plastic horseshoe keychain that I had enjoyed owning. I asked him to bring it back to me on his return. I guess in my naiveté I thought that if he had to bring it back to me, nothing would happen to him.

Uncle James and that keepsake survived the fierce fighting on the islands of the Pacific where he had many close calls. He kept it in the pocket over his heart, he said. Returning, he placed in my hand the battered, misshaped plastic keychain that had gone through the war with him. I still treasure it, for it reminds me of our shared love and respect.

He also gave me one of his Navy woolen sailor middies that I (as an early teenager) wore proudly with a white pleated skirt and saddle oxfords. I remember we were required to remove his official Naval emblems, patches, rank, and name before I could wear it.

Throat problems of hoarseness, hard breathing, infections, and dilations on my narrow trachea obviously limited my physical activity. I did enjoy walking, roller-skating, and bicycling from time to time. The padded basket on the front handlebars of my bike allowed my fox terrier, Lady, to accompany me on errands or when riding with friends.

Reading through the many types of books in my school library, I came across one entitled "A MAN CALLED PETER."[23] It was not about the Peter in the Bible as I had expected, but I read it anyway. I was captivated when I read that because God loves us, He plants dreams in our hearts to grow like seeds, until the time for fulfillment is right. Then to our surprise we discover God's will and ours are the same.[24] I asked God right then to plant His dreams in my heart. In a church service soon after, I dedicated myself to definite Christian service, possibly to be a missionary, if that is where the Lord led.

Through my church I attended camps, first as participant and later as counselor. I was privileged to attend Southern Baptist Training Union Conventions as a teen, visiting Kentucky colleges en route, thus birthing a college dream. When I was 15, I competed in the annual teen Sword Drill of finding verses and books in the Bible rapidly and accurately, becoming runner-up for the State of Kentucky.

To school and church activities, at 16 I added part-time

jobs in the summers and during Christmas. In an all-girls high school (not made coed until 1950) I donned the popular saddle oxfords, bobby socks and flared skirts. Like other teens I was buffeted by the winds of change, trapped in the sandbars of fear, and challenged by the waves of the future.

Dating gradually changed from going to the local drugstore for a soda with two straws, to our biking to one of the three large parks surrounding Louisville. Other times the-boy-of-the-moment and I swished along in autumn leaves, or listened to the snow crunch beneath our feet. We usually rode streetcars (until buses replaced them) downtown to the movie theater, the ice skating rink, roller derbies, circuses, and ballets. On rare occasions my date and I strolled all the way downtown and across the Second Street bridge over the Ohio River, and back, a distance of six miles or so.

Midst the virtual sunlight of my teen years, new golden dreams arose – a dream of going to Georgetown College (KY) – a dream of being a teacher or maybe a scientist – a dream of marrying a minister or becoming a missionary. The words of Jesus, "You are the light of the world"[25] fueled my dreams of letting others know Jesus loves them. As the Lord enlightened my search for Him during my teen years, my faith, now lit, began its slow descent from my head to become trust in my heart.

SCRIPTURES and NOTES

17 Genesis 1:3
Then God said, Let there be light and there was light.

18 Genesis 1:16-17,19
Then God made two great lights: the greater light to rule the day, and the lesser light to rule the night. He made the stars also. God set them in the firmament of the heavens to give light on the earth. So the evening and the morning were the fourth day.

19 John 8:12
Then Jesus spoke to them again, saying, I am the light of the world. He who follows Me shall not walk in darkness, but have the light of life.

20 Psalm 104:1-2
Bless the Lord, O my soul! O Lord my God, You are very great: You are clothed with honor and majesty, who cover Yourself with light as with a garment, who stretch out the heavens like a curtain.

21 Revelation 22:16
I, Jesus, have sent My angel to testify to you these things in the churches. I am the Root and the Offspring of David, the Bright and Morning Star.

22 John 1:8-9
He (John) was not that Light, but was sent to bear witness of that Light. That was the true Light which gives light to every man coming into the world.

23 Catherine Marshall, A MAN CALLED PETER, (New York: McGraw-Hill, 1951).

24 Catherine Marshall, A MAN CALLED PETER, (New York: McGraw-Hill, 1951), p 59.

25 Matthew 5:14
You are the light of the world. A city that is set on a hill cannot be hidden.

GREEN
The Color of Power

Green must have been a favorite choice of God in the creation of earth. He lavishly used myriad shades to color His land, sea, and sky. Verdant hues are seen worldwide during storms, in water, and in plants.

Green, a secondary color dependent upon yellow and blue, is defined as healing and restful, and indicates life and growth. Since life and growth are only possible through the Lord's power, the obvious color choice for His power is green. The Lord has the definitive green thumb, for the power of growth is His, whether in the natural realm or the spiritual. King David proclaimed, "Yours, O Lord, is the greatness, the power and the glory, . . . In Your hand is power and might."[26]

God unfolded His plan for me just as He opens a new green leaf, gradually and purposely. Walking in His light through my teens had been new and exciting. Consequently, my faith was still shining through the yellow light of caution. Wanting to grow me from "eye arresting" yellow to "eye resting" green, the Lord gave a resounding "Yes" to my dream of going away to college. My heart's desire culminated in being able to go to Georgetown College, a Southern Baptist College in the heart of the Kentucky bluegrass, with a scholarship and work-ship!

Removed 70 miles from home and the familiar, as a "greenhorn" freshman in 1950 I watched how others dealt with joy, fatigue, fear, and frustrations. We prayed in groups and privately about everything. We asked God specifically to show us what we should major in to prepare us for serving Him.

Once again the Lord used visions to show me His plan. The first involved one of my favorite pictures, painted by Warner Sallman, "The Lord Is My Shepherd." The Good Shepherd, Jesus, in white is carrying a lamb as He leads a flock of sheep on a grassy slope near a river with mountains behind. In my vision the Lord brought this scene to life. I watched the Lord walk, leading the sheep, heard the river ripple and felt the soft breeze. He stopped and knelt among the flock that was occasionally bleating. Then He lifted up a lamb slightly above His head at arms' length. A ray of light from heaven shone on the lamb and through the lamb to the sheep surrounding Him. I understood somehow that I was that lamb and would let His light shine through me as a teacher. As a result, I majored in elementary education. Still wanting to serve the Lord through music, I chose it for my minor.

In the second vision I found myself in a room where hundreds of framed pictures of Christ in all sizes and views totally covered the walls from ceiling to floor. I had never seen most of these pictures before, but they dominated the room. Upon awakening I felt in awe of His lingering presence, preoccupied with the impression that the Lord must be first in my life. Because He was so real to me, I wanted to learn how to love Him with all my heart, mind, soul, and strength.[27] A worthy goal, to be sure, but growth takes the Lord's power, His timing, and more experiences, not just desire.

Finding science courses a source of joy, I took them as electives. My professor, Dr. H. Y. Mullikin, urged me to major in science, and to seek my life's work in that field. Now I faced a dilemma. I still wanted to marry a minister and serve the Lord ministering to people. Would working in scientific research in labs or astronomy be compatible with my goals? Would there always be jobs available? This unexpected turn of events sent me back to the Lord, who, by giving me no further word, obviously meant for me to continue in what He had already shown me.

In nature, we know that seeds, soil, rain, and sun are just separate entities. Though the seeds contain a germ of life within, they are unable to produce on their own. When the seeds are planted, watered, and sunned, they become infused by the Lord's power and sprout into roots and new green shoots.

My separate entities included graduating from college ready to teach, trained to play piano and organ, still single, and needing a job. Growth does not happen because all the elements are in place, but because of the Lord's power. Ambition, though embedded in the seeds, must be tempered with His power in His time. My green sprout of trust took root by starting with faith in the Lord, then shot upward toward the light by striving to achieve, as if it were all up to me.

SCRIPTURES and NOTES

26 1 Chronicles 29:11-12

Yours, O Lord, is the greatness, the power and the glory, the victory and the majesty; for all that is in heaven and in earth is Yours; Yours is the kingdom, O Lord, and You are exalted as head over all.

Both riches and honor come from You, and You reign over all. In Your hand is power and might; in Your hand it is to make great and to give strength to all.

27 Luke 10:27

So He answered and said, You shall love the Lord your God with all your heart, with all your soul, with all your strength, and with all your mind, and your neighbor as yourself.

BLUE
The Color of Truth

Blue is cool and calming, different from the excitement of red and the enlightenment of yellow. Blue is a dichotomy in that it is both authoritative and retreating. It commands attention in uniforms, and designates handicap parking places and hospitals. Yet blue retreats, making it perfectly suited for backgrounds and moods.

The down side of our emotions is expressed by "the blues," pressing time into slow motion as it sinks us into the deeper waters of melancholy and depression. Writers capture our gloominess, and musicians wail with a beat the depths of our sadness.

The up side of blue is expressed by honoring winners with blue ribbons, preferring blue-chip stocks, and desiring blue diamonds. The Creator Himself prompted us to think of blue as a spiritual color by choosing to make the heavens high above us blue. The Lord designated blue as one of the colors to be used in the Tabernacle,[28] after He had sprinkled the blue planet with blue flowers, birds, whales, gems, and foods.

Blue, which cannot be made from other colors, stands alone the way truth does. The very first word in the Hebrew Bible is "Elohim"[29] ("El" meaning strong, "Oh" truth, "IM" plural three) and is translated as Lord God Almighty. Inherent in the Father, Son and Holy Spirit are truth and strength.[30] There is an ancient Jewish prayer that says:

From the cowardice that shrinks from new truth,
From the laziness that is content with half-truth,
From the arrogance that thinks it knows all truth,
O God of truth, deliver us.

Truth is strength-in-control. Truth is the basic ingredient of integrity moving us toward purity, loyalty, endurance, and trust.

Standing on the threshold of adulthood, I faced the inevitable truth of needing a job and a place to live. Not being very brave, I applied to teach in Louisville, desiring to live at home. Hired by the Board of Education for the grand sum of $2800.00 in 1953, I became a third grade teacher at Hazelwood Elementary. Teaching those 36 loving, eager pupils made my first year a blue ribbon experience of fun and fulfillment. Starting out to perpetuate in them such qualities as honesty, fairness, ambition, and hope, I became overwhelmed with the truth that God really did call me to teach and that I enjoyed it. I had become that lamb in my dreams, and was allowing His light to shine through me.

I taught first, second or third grade for the next 11 years. In spite of a weak throat that was frequently hoarse, I loved teaching. Because I was often reduced to whispering, my students had to be quiet to hear me, making my class the quietest in the school. Swinging between the exhilaration of teaching and the exhaustion, I was stretched to my limits – the perfect prerequisites for growth.

As I have stated, Bible reading and a prayer time were unscheduled activities during my teens. After re-dedications I would faithfully engage in daily devotional times for a while, then taper off again to hardly ever. I remember thinking, when I get in college, I will do better. In college, I thought, it will be different when I am working. So it was – not by choice – but because I ran out of steam and was driven often to my knees to survive.

Another dream came to fulfillment when I was 25 and in my fifth year of teaching. That autumn I asked a seminary friend, Les Werner, if he could introduce me to any of his single preacher friends. Later on campus, a seminary friend asked Les if he knew anyone unattached he could meet. Les and Evelyn arranged and accompanied us on a blind date to go bowling on January 18, 1958. My date, Norval Lee Bard, was preparing to be a minister and was already a trained soloist. He was 6'2 with hazel-green eyes and a receding hairline (which, incidentally, did not bother me at all because my daddy whom I adored was bald).

After three dates, Norval returned to the St. Louis area for several months. He said he would write, but not daily because he had done that and found it to be tiresome. Intuitively I knew if our dating were to continue, he would have to initiate the timing and the progress. Purposely, I wrote him only in answer to his letters. If he took two or three weeks to write, then I waited two or three weeks before answering. Consequently I have a total of seven letters from him between February and August!

He came back to Louisville for a visit on Memorial Day weekend. During a picnic to Shawnee Park while he was waxing his car, I told the Lord privately that if this was the man He wanted me to marry, it was fine with me. I added that He would have to make it happen. Of course I said nothing to Norval about this, who was also saying nothing. The truth of the matter is we had not even held hands yet, but passed the hours together talking, getting to know one another.

In early June he returned for my daddy's funeral and the weekend. By the end of August Norval moved back to Louisville to resume seminary, and to find out how he felt about me (so he told me later). I never forgot the thrill the first time he reached over to hold my hand, starting our tradition of handholding for the next 38 years. By the time he got around to kissing me goodnight, I was hopelessly in love. In October he gave me an emerald-cut diamond for my birthday, creatively framing his proposal as if he were reading our wedding announcement. We married in Victory Memorial Baptist Church 11 months after we met. My three attendants wore pale green, Gone-With-The-Wind-type dresses. The "something blue," a lacy garter I wore during the ceremony, was a hidden witness to our promises to be true to each other "until death do us part."

Still teaching full time, I earned a Master of Education degree from the University of Louisville by 1960. Norval graduated from the Southern Baptist Seminary with a Bachelor of Divinity in January 1962, (later upgraded to a Master of Divinity). We were both prepared and ready to follow the Lord wherever He might lead. He had heard our prayers and fulfilled our dreams of education, music, and marriage. Now new goals of a pastorate and children emerged.

At the time of my daddy's death, I learned of his tremendous witness to his fellow workers. He let them know that Jesus loved them and cared about them. He showed them by example how to walk with the Lord. He listened to their problems and prayed for them. He did this individually and privately, never telling anyone, not even his family. He was counted as a friend both by believers and non-believers alike. I had seen my daddy's deep love for His Lord through the years, and now I knew he revealed it by unashamedly loving and ministering to others.

His example stirred me to respond to my inner longing to know the Lord better. In private, I re-affirmed that Jesus Christ was my Savior and Lord. I vowed to seek Him first, and to make my Bible study a pursuit with purpose. The seed of spiritual growth planted by my parents and church had finally rooted and sprouted into a lifetime goal; rooted in the Living and the Written Word, and sprouted in His ministering to others through me. A sky-high, true-blue commitment, indeed!

The truth is, I would pass through many shades and moods of blue in my learning to trust. As the primary colors of red, yellow and blue provide the depths from which all colors are created, the love, light, and truth of the Lord provide the depths from which all spiritual growth is possible.

SCRIPTURES and NOTES

28 Numbers 4:6-7, 11

Then they shall put on it a covering of badger skins, and spread over that a cloth entirely of blue; and they shall insert its poles.

On the table of showbread they shall spread a blue cloth, and put on it the dishes, the pans, the bowls, and the pitchers for pouring; and the showbread shall be on it.

Over the golden altar they shall spread a blue cloth, and cover it with a covering of badger skins; and they shall insert its poles.

29 Genesis 1:1

In the beginning God created the heavens and the earth.

(Hebrew: God created heavens and earth in beginning.)

30 John 15:26

But when the Helper comes, whom I shall send to you from the Father, the Spirit of Truth who proceeds from the Father, He will testify of Me.

INDIGO
The Color of Holiness

Indigo is the name of a plant that in the past was grown mainly in India. It was used to dye cotton and wool a blue so deep that it took on a purplish cast. As time passed the plant's name came to mean the distinctive color of the dye. Though indigo is now produced synthetically, the color name survives.

The deep midnight blue of the rainbow slides into indigo, a dark secondary color. Indigo, beyond the blue of truth, seems recessive, perfect for reflective thinking about God and life and goals. Some of life's hardest questions come unbidden, such as, Who am I? Why am I here? Is God real? Why does He allow evil?

As indigo is not static, neither do these questions stop. Accepting the truth that "God is"[31] lets us glimpse into one of His less obvious qualities, holiness. One of His names is "Jehovah-M'Kaddesh," meaning God is holy.[32] Scriptures teach us that the Lord is to be revered and honored,[33] but learning how takes time and experience.

With dreams intact of success in the ministry, Norval accepted the call to a small church south of Chicago. Northern Illinois was considered a pioneer area for Southern Baptist work in the early 1960s. Churches were small and the work was hard. We self-moved our stuff, plants, and pets. Though five months pregnant, I helped redecorate a rented three-bedroom house since the church had no parsonage. We rejoiced over the new pastorate, and the new baby's pending arrival.

Our son was born in 1963, bringing us much joy. We had to move and repaint five times during the next two years because all rentals were repossessed houses, available for only a part of a year. As our income was unavoidably small, Norval and I both became substitute teachers, and I taught private piano lessons.

Even though we prayed and worked hard, there seemed to be an unresolved power struggle within the church. My husband finally resigned as Pastor after two years. Once again, I was five months pregnant. Our dreams turned to hard-nosed reality as we faced the prospect of no regular income and no place to live. While we prayed, sent resumes, and sought advice from friends, Norval painted houses and did all kinds of odd jobs to help us survive.

After our daughter was born in 1965, we were invited to live rent-free in an older parsonage of another church. We lived there for several months until Norval was called as full-time Pastor of a small church north of Chicago. He also taught seventh and eighth grade English and social studies in the local public school. During this pastorate our second daughter was born in 1968. I continued to teach private piano and organ to help make ends meet.

With doing the church bulletins, music, and teaching a class each Sunday, plus caring for three pre-schoolers, I grew weary. Often I struggled with my weak, hoarse throat, requiring medicine we could ill afford. One of our girls was allergic to about a third of God's creation and needed regular shots. We found it very expensive to live near Chicago, and prayed for both relief and guidance. Our best efforts to provide extra income barely kept our heads above water – an indigo situation, for sure!

In the summer of 1969, I set up a corner place for my private, early morning devotions with a small table, a folding chair, my Bible, a notebook, and candle. As I daily lit the candle, I remembered that Christ was the light of the world.[34] Watching the candle burn, I thought of other similarities, and wrote the following in my prayer journal:

> *I am the wick, my world the candle. There is only one wick per candle. My task is to let the light and fire of Christ burn in me and through me to make a difference in those surrounding me. The wick does not move as the fire burns. Likewise the Holy Spirit keeps the wick-*

me still so He can use me, and change me. The black residue in the melted wax pictures with visible ugliness the burning of the Holy Spirit as He rids me of sins.

When the candle is lit, the wax at the top is hard. The fire melts the wax nearest the wick first. After a while, it is warmed and pliable.

The melted wax, in constant motion at the top of candle, is like those around me, busy as beavers in their "go-go" world. Those closest to me should feel the Lord's presence first, and be melted, and warmed toward my Savior.

As the fire burns, the circle of melted wax grows larger and larger until the wax overflows its sides, and cascades down the candle. The ideal is for my circle to widen until the Lord's light and warmth is felt by the most distant person I know, clear to the bottom of the candle where it's dark and cold.

Once after an impossible week of guests and sicknesses I penned, *"No time for private devotions last week. Forgive me, Lord. And now, today I cannot even light the candle because my matches are upstairs. Without our daily time together, I feel unlit too, as if my Light were upstairs or far away."*

At the end of five years Norval felt led to resign. Desiring specific guidance, we put out a fleece (like Gideon did in the Old Testament).[35] We told the Lord that if He sold our house by August 31, 1970, that would be the sign we were to leave the area. We repainted where needed and waited all summer. Our realtor assured us no houses were selling, but we continued to wait on the Lord. The last week of August a man from the Midwest who had been newly hired as a professor in a nearby college, looked at our house along with others for sale. At 3 p.m. on August 31, he bought ours with the condition that we be out within the next week before his family and furniture arrived. We packed and moved as agreed.

Norval drove a rented moving truck, pulling a trailer. I

followed in our car with children and pets, likewise pulling a trailer. We covered about 500 miles to get to western Kentucky where Norval had relatives. We went from suburban living to rural "roughing-it." In the old, two-story farmhouse, water was hand-pumped into the kitchen from the cistern. Each room was heated by a fireplace that mixed smoke with heat. We borrowed a wringer washer and strung clotheslines from tree to tree. We signed up our son, age seven, for the rural school and bus route. We lived there during the fall months and enjoyed it immensely. No one in our family even caught a cold during this time.

By December Norval was called as associate pastor to a church in town, and we moved into their second parsonage. Our son had to change schools, but our daughter could now go to school. We were pleased to take her to kindergarten at the Presbyterian church that my husband's great-grandfather, Isaac Bard, had started in the 1800's. It was good for us and our children to be with family, in the area of Bard lands, family cemetery, and homes.

Our indigo times helped us to better worship the Lord the way He deserves. We allowed Him to minister to us and through us. We had weathered the storms of no house, no job, and no prospects – places where following the Lord led us to deeper revelations of His sacred Holiness. It is almost impossible to separate who God is from what He does, but there is no doubt that holiness is inherent in the Lord's nature.

Since spiritual growth was on the Lord's agenda for me, I was to find that problems and crises were really opportunities to increase my trust in Him. Experiencing life, day by day, imperceptibly moved me from the blue of His truth into the indigo of His holiness.

SCRIPTURES and NOTES

31 Exodus 3:14

And God said to Moses, "AM WHO I AM (Jehovah). And He said, Thus you shall say to the children of Israel, I AM has sent me to you.

32 Leviticus 19:1-2

And the Lord spoke to Moses, saying,

Speak to all the congregation of the children of Israel, and say to them: You shall be holy, for I am holy.

33 Psalm 29:1-2

Give unto the Lord, O you mighty ones, give unto the Lord glory and strength. Give unto the Lord the glory due to His name; worship the Lord in the beauty of holiness.

34 John 8:12

Then Jesus spoke to them again, saying, I am the light of the world. He who follows Me shall not walk in darkness, but have the light of life.

35 Judges 6:36-40

So Gideon said to God, If You will save Israel by my hand as You have said –

Look, I shall put a fleece of wool on the threshing floor; if there is dew on the fleece only, and it is dry on all the ground, then I shall know that You will save Israel by my hand, as You have said. And it was so.

When he rose early the next morning and squeezed the fleece together, he wrung the dew out of the fleece, a bowlful of water.

Then Gideon said to God, Do not be angry with me, but let me speak just once more: Let me test, I pray, just once more with the fleece; let it now be dry only on the fleece, but on all the ground let there be dew.

And God did so that night. It was dry on the fleece only, but there was dew on all the ground.

VIOLET
The Color of Kingship

Violet combines blue with red, completing the basic rainbow colors. It is synonymous with purple and signifies royalty. Violet became known as the color of kings because only rich kings could afford to own deep, purple-dyed garments. It is no surprise that the Lord said to use purple in the tabernacle.[36] It is emblematic of authority, power, justice, and wisdom, all pointing to the Kingship of our Lord.

Incidentally, the lion, known as the "king of beasts," was the symbol for the tribe of Judah.[37] Jesus Christ is called "the Lion of the tribe of Judah."[38] With the blue of His truth and red of His love blended perfectly, our Lord will return to reign forever as King.[39]

Learning how to respect, adore and worship "El Elyon," the God Most High,[40] does not come overnight or just because of desire. Rather it's a growing process. We move on from His truth, holiness and righteousness into the reigning, royal reality of the King of Kings.[41]

Our reverence for the Christ the King grew as Norval and I experienced the ups and downs of pastoring, parenting, and progressing through the stages of life.

We left Kentucky after three-and-a-half years and returned to Illinois in the dead of winter. This time we moved to his inheritance, a house in a small town in southern Illinois where Norval had spent his childhood and youth. Though it was only two bedrooms, we used the children's furniture as partitions and found a spot each of us could call his own. Work for Norval in the area was practically non-existent, so a neighbor and the local church supplied us with food and heating fuel. Ironically, we did not qualify for food stamps because my mother was making our car payments.

Three months later Norval was called as pastor of a small church about 40 miles away. He also served as substitute teacher for the county schools in that area. We felt we had come home for we loved ministering through the church again, and living in their small town. However, due to our moving twice, our fifth and third graders ended up changing schools three times that year.

I served as church pianist or organist and continued teaching music to my own three. I added to our income by teaching piano, organ, or guitar chords to other youths there. One of my goals as a church musician has always been to train and leave qualified pianists or organists at each place. I taught hymns as well as the basics and classical music, delving into theory and harmony playing. The students gained experience by performing with me for services when they had something ready. One of the teens then whose heart's desire was to play for her church continues to do so after all these years. What a joy! – To be able to serve through music and help others achieve the same goals.

After four years we moved to Carbondale, home of Southern Illinois University. Norval promised our children that the family would stay put until all three had graduated from high school. Norval supplemented our income by working in the local tape factory. He served as pastor of a small church about 60 miles away, driving up and back on Sundays. The children and I attended a local church except for the rare occasions when we went with Norval. I again taught music to local pupils.

When our older children left for college, we augmented our income by renting their bedrooms to foreign students who wanted to live in an American home. We were blessed by those visiting and living in our home, for we learned about foreign cultures and customs. We were able to share from time to time God's love for the whole world through His Son, Jesus.[42] The only negative side of this marvelous arrangement was when our children came home at vacation times. They had to camp out in the living room and den because strangers were living in their rooms.

The "for richer or poorer" side of our marriage vows always seemed to lean heavy on the poorer end. We survived because the Lord provided the basics of food, clothing and shelter by one means or another. It was a special treat for our family to be able to eat at McDonald's or to celebrate a birthday in a "pizza pie parlor." Traditional values of honesty, hard work, family unity, and spiritual growth were taught and practiced.

Throughout the years, it seemed we frequently had to leave friends we had grown to love in that community. We also said good-bye permanently to the older generation, one by one, as they left us.

The "in sickness and in health promises" were pushed to the limit during this time by throat surgery necessitating my wearing a "trach" for four years, and later I needed a hysterectomy.

"For better and for worse, until death do us part" was a promise we kept for 38 years before Norval was killed in a pedestrian accident. On our 37th anniversary, Norval gave me a homemade card on which he had written, "We've had some rough years, but never a bad one." Like all couples, we had our ups and downs as we continued to grow and change. Through our shared experiences, we learned more about our Lord and each other.

As time passed, I came to depend more and more on my Lord. I expressed to Him my adoration, worship, and thanks. I prayed for those near and far, and I prayed for myself, that the Lord would change me, that He would mold me for His purposes.

Having "prayer journaled" the old-fashioned way with pen and paper for years, I joined the computer age after we moved to South Carolina. I began to type out my honest thoughts and feelings to the Lord through the computer. I asked Him how He saw the problem, and if there was anything He wanted to say at that time. I sat quietly and waited. When the Lord responded with His calm, authoritative voice, time faded as I became aware of His eternal, overwhelming presence. I heard His actual words inside as clearly as if they were spoken aloud. His words are different from my thoughts, offering challenge, yet satisfying my heart completely.

The measure of faith He gave me to start with grew into a beanstalk of trust, not overnight as in the fairy tale, but with each experience. My faith has been pushed to its limits in the areas of marriage, health, finances, relatives, parenting, widowhood, and writing. I write what the Lord has shown me and done for me, hoping it will encourage others to seek the King of Kings, the One-Who-Reigns,[43] the God Most High.

I am glad the Lord used a colorful panorama to teach me about Him. The rainbow's basic colors have communicated seven attributes of our Lord; namely, love, forgiveness, light, power, truth, holiness, and kingship. It is true, the seven basic colors are what I already knew about Him, but I have spent a lifetime getting to know Him better, experience by experience.

In the following chapters, the new shades of colors tell of unique times in which dependence on the Lord was my only hope for solution, for survival, for the supernatural. That He has loved me through it all, and still does, is my security. Learning to trust the Lord, no matter what, is not easy, as you will see.

SCRIPTURES and NOTES

36 Exodus 26:1

Moreover, you shall make the tabernacle with ten curtains of fine woven linen, and blue, purple and scarlet threads; with artistic designs of cherubim you shall weave them.

37 Genesis 49:9

Judah is a lion's whelp; from the prey, my son, you have gone up. He bows down, he lies down as a lion; and as a lion, who shall rouse him?

38 Revelation 5:5

But one of the elders said to me, Do not weep, Behold, the Lion of the tribe of Judah, the Root of David, has prevailed to open the scroll and to loose its seven seals.

39 Psalm 29:10

The Lord sat enthroned at the Flood, and the Lord sits as King forever.

40 Genesis 14:18-19

Then Melchizedek king of Salem brought out bread and wine; he was the priest of God Most High.

And he blessed him and said: Blessed be Abram of God Most High, Possessor of heaven and earth; and blessed be God Most High Who has delivered your enemies into your hand.

41 Revelations 19:16

And He has on His robe and on His thigh a name written: KINGS OF KINGS and LORD OF LORDS.

42 John 3:16

For God so loved the world that He gave His only begotten Son, that whoever believes in Him should not perish but have everlasting life.

43 Psalm 47:2

For the Lord Most High is awesome; He is a great King over all the earth.

BETWEEN

THE

BASIC

COLORS

SAPPHIRE
The Color of Faithfulness

A sapphire is a bright blue gem that is transparent. "On a clear day you can see forever" connotes a sapphire blue sky to me. It is a true blue, a rich color pulling you into its depths, the way truth does. Truth in any discipline lures us to plumb its depths. If something eludes us, we push on to find the truth, to find what is missing. In the matter of religion, I was a believer, a devoted follower of Christ, who prayed and studied the Bible daily, yet I felt something was missing. I wanted something more, prayed often about my feeling incomplete, and sought to find solutions.

After 22 years the mirage of our picture-perfect marriage had gradually faded into the domination of rights or needs uppermost at the moment. We still loved each other, but daily living had ground underfoot our rose-colored ideals.

In addition, our home life was worn thin with our teenagers' school projects, dental appointments, and schedules of ball, music, and church activities. Into this patchwork of confusion were sewn pastoral responsibilities, sibling conflicts, my struggles with a weak throat, and three under-foot housedogs. To finish the evening meal without the phone's ringing, friends' arriving, or schedules' interfering was a rare occurrence. Living in our family was chaotic at best, usually registering at the upper end of the stress scale.

In the fall of 1980, John and Loretta Wittmer, casual friends, stopped by for a visit, and told us about a retreat for pastors and wives they had attended six months before in Titusville, Florida. "This conference was a life-changing experience for us," John said. "Oh, you must plan to go," urged Loretta, "whether or not you have any problems."

It's a good thing they don't know us well or they would probably insist we go! I thought to myself but I said, "We cannot afford a weekend in the next town, not to mention going from Illinois to Florida!"

"Your only cost is the $25.00 registration fee," John responded. "The church sponsors and staffs a retreat center and provides buses for the trip as one of the annual ministries of the Park Avenue Baptist Church for pastors and deacons. If you are interested, you had better send in your reservations now and get on the waiting list, because there is a limit of about 50 couples for each of the three weeks."

"But what would we do about our three teenagers?" Norval countered. "We cannot be away for 10 days."

"Ask the Lord to send someone to stay in your home," Loretta suggested. "Then start asking around to find out whom He is going to send."

After they left, I said to Norval, "There must be more to life than what I am finding. Where is the joy, the abounding, the soaring I've dreamed of and read about? Life is so difficult – so filled with . . . duties," I finally stammered; but I was thinking . . .if my family acted differently, my life would not be such an uphill battle. Aloud I continued, "Do you think this conference is that unusual?"

"There is no way to know unless we give it a try," he replied. "Anyway, we have nothing to lose."

We applied and were placed on standby; in January our reservations were confirmed. For the 10-day trip south, we needed both winter and spring clothes, the latter still boxed from having moved on January 1. God did provide an adult brave enough to stay with our teenagers.

On a Thursday night in February we boarded the chartered bus, leaving ice and snow behind for the land of promise in the sunny south. We collapsed on the seats and slept fitfully to the rhythm of the rolling road. During the next day Norval wandered up and down the bus aisle enjoying the new people. As I was extremely tired and had a hoarse throat, I sat quietly, staring out my window at the panorama of bleak winter scenes.

Arriving Saturday afternoon, Norval and I were assigned to room 1 Thessalonians 5:24 in the retreat center. "Dif ferent from just numbers," I said. The first thing I did upon entering our room was to look up the verse, which reads, "Faithful is He who calls you, who also will do it." As we moved in and dressed for dinner we wondered aloud what the verse meant, and why we were assigned that room.

Beginning at the Saturday night meeting, the retreaters sang to autoharp accompaniment...that is, all except me. I wanted to sing but was still hoarse. Since I could not participate the way the others did, my frustrations spun into anger. I sought out staff counselor Danny for help. "Do you have any idea why I would be angry just because I cannot sing with the others?" I asked.

He returned, "What does God want you to do?"

"I thought I was supposed to sing," I said in a raspy voice.

Danny responded, "Would God demand something of you that you cannot do right now?"

"Well – no, I guess not, but what should I do?"

"Let us ask the Lord what He wants you to do," he said. We bowed our heads and he prayed aloud for guidance. God immediately gave him several options – humming, listening, whistling, mouthing the words – options which would release my unreal expectations and defuse the anger.

As we talked further, I expressed my longing to soar as a Christian. Danny continued, "Since prayer is two-way communication, have you spoken to the Lord about this lack you feel? Did you wait right then for His response?"

"No, I guess not. Even when I've prayed about it, I guess 'I' have decided what 'I' thought God wanted me to do."

"Self has to die," Danny pointed out, "not be rededicated or made more confident, in order for Christ to reign in you.[44] Denying Him this right may have left your soul running on empty. The 'something more' you're seeking probably lies in this realm."

"It sounds like I need a change inside," I said to Danny, "but how can I change when I do not know what needs changing?"

"Only God knows that. Ask Him," he advised in conclusion.

I mumbled going down the hall, "Now I am more confused than ever. Haven't I spent years praying? Asking? Anyway how can I tell whether He is speaking, or it's just my thoughts?"

Desiring privacy, I returned to our room. My shaking knees readily knelt at the foot of the bed, glad to be relieved of their responsibility. Pouring out my inner turmoil, I prayed aloud,

> *Lord! I am puzzled, . . . and scared. Forgive me for deciding what I thought You wanted me to do, and for my doing all the talking at prayer time. From now on You are in charge, and I will listen for Your voice.*
>
> *In a few days, I will be leaving here and I need a relationship with You that will sustain me. I do not want to go back home empty inside. Would You show me something about You, Lord, that will help me now, and later?*

My mind has never understood what happened next, but my unbelieving eyes focused on the word G O D in bold, black letters entering a prism as a beam of light. His name emerged on the other side as a rainbow of the seven basic colors, so vibrant it appeared to be alive. Awestruck, I saw the seven colors spread apart, showing an empty space between each. As I watched, an infinite number of graduating shades filled up the spaces between the basic colors. When finished, I could no longer determine the original color bands. I now saw an enlarged, energized rainbow of perfectly blended hues.[45]

"God, that's beautiful," I whispered, "but what does it mean?"

After a timeless moment of majestic silence, His inaudible voice spoke,

> The seven basic colors are what you already know about Me. . . love, forgiveness, light, power, truth, holiness, and kingship. The new shades of colors are what you are going to learn about Me in the future. Just as the added shades are impossible

to number, neither will you ever know all about Me.

"Thank You, Lord," I hoarsely uttered at last in amazement. Not wanting this moment to escape without getting all I was seeking, I hesitantly prayed,

> *Lord, I need help not only for my inner self, but as a wife and mother. I do not know what needs to be changed inside of me, or how to go about it if I did. Would You show me something about myself that will help me in the days ahead?*

The rainbow receded, as a picture of the linoleum on my kitchen floor appeared. I could see plainly the pattern of the large irregular patio stones in grays and greens held in place by concrete-looking mortar. Then the Lord said,

> You become locked into predictable patterns and safe situations that give you false security. I AM your security. Let Me flow through you, making you flexible and fluid and free from yourself.
>
> Change is painful, but necessary for growth. In every instance, give Me the problem or the injustice you feel; you do not have to be tense inside, or have word-fights to prove you are right.
>
> Seeing My sufficiency within will lead you to be an overcomer, even in moments of intense distress. You will fail sometimes, since perfection belongs to Me alone. When you do, remember I love you – just the way I made you. I AM helping you to become the person I planned for you to be when I created you.

Suddenly the linoleum image was gone, and so was the heaviness that had entered the room with me. With praise and gratitude, I rose from my knees with the "something more" in my heart, . . . and awed that the Lord God Almighty had responded to me. With these teachings and personal pictures indelibly imprinted, I could face the future with hope. My feet hardly seemed to touch the ground as I left to find Norval and tell him what I had seen and learned.

We returned to Illinois eager to let the Lord of the rainbow reign within to change us, for we were filled with the possibilities of "Faithful is He who calls you, who also will do it."[46]

The retreat experience was life changing for us. But our marriage box still contained puzzle pieces with the rough edges of who we were. Back in Illinois we quickly slid into familiar routines. Our first impasse came a few days later when Norval and I were putting up cornice boards in our bedroom.

"Are you planning to attach the supports perpendicular to the window facings?" I had asked, implying (I guess) I knew how a carpenter might do it.

"No, I am not," Norval had replied. "I thought I would run them parallel to the window at the height needed."

"Then how can you be sure they will be level with the window all the way across?" I returned.

"By measuring and marking," he answered, "but I am not going to fight with you about this. To make you happy I will do it your way." And he did!

Winning a disagreement this way did not make me happy, but left me feeling disturbed. As soon as possible I sought a private place and asked the Lord who was right, and why peace had fled. No answer . . .

Two days later when I was at the sewing machine, that Majestic, Eternity-filled Voice spoke,

> It does not matter who was right and who was wrong. Whether you win or lose is not the issue. You are to nurture your husband by supporting him every chance you get. That way you help him to achieve My goals for him.
>
> Allow My love to keep on changing you, and flowing through you to your family continually.

Excitement pulsed through me as I thanked God for His help. The Lord was changing me inside, showing me how to relate to my family in His love, not in my strength. "Faithful is He who calls you, who also will do it" was becoming real to me.

I knew in my head that the Lord had been faithful to me all my life, but now my heart knew that truth. One day it dawned on me that "faithfulness" had to be the first new shade in the rainbow that the Lord was teaching me about Himself. Clear as a sapphire is the truth that the Lord is faithful.[47]

SCRIPTURES and NOTES

44 Galatians 2:20

I have been crucified with Christ; it is no longer I who live, but Christ lives in me; and the life which I now live in the flesh I live by faith in the Son of God, who love me and gave himself for me.

45 Ezekiel 1:28

Like the appearance of a rainbow in a cloud on a rainy day, so was the appearance of the brightness all around it. This was the appearance of the likeness of the glory of the Lord.

46 1 Thessalonians 5:24

47 2 Thessalonians 3:3

But the Lord is faithful, who shall stablish you, and keep you from evil.

BITTERSWEET
The Color of Shepherding

Inherent in bittersweet are red and yellow, with strong leanings toward the red. The red of love and the yellow of enlightenment produce the orange of forgiveness as already seen in the first three colors of the rainbow. A loving, enlightened heart overshadows wrongdoings, and offers forgiveness. However, this "burnt orange" forgiveness is best because it is heavy with love, completely without retribution or remembering. Such is the heart of God and His Son, Jesus,[48] the Good Shepherd,[49] who is so glad to find a lost or straying sheep (like me) that all is forgiven in His loving welcome.[50]

It was easy to trust God when our marriage was new, and my husband was finishing seminary. We felt like able engineers on a train of trust. We rode full speed ahead on tracks laid by God, stretching into a rosy future.

Our first pastorate was limited in size and finances, causing my husband to become a bi-vocational pastor. This is the equivalent of one engineer personally keeping the three fully loaded, parallel trains of church, job, and home going at the same speed and progress.

Over the next several years the home train grew in length as a passenger car was added for each of our three children. Freight cars were needed for basic furniture and appliances, baggage cars for overloaded budgets and time, and cattle cars for pets. Boxcars moved us to new places. Refrigerated cars were for things on hold. We prayed about everything and believed we were on the right track. We still considered ourselves able engineers, thus unintentionally keeping Christ in the caboose along with deeper spiritual matters.

Finally, after 10 years of pastorates in Illinois and Kentucky, ending with three months of no employment, we invited Christ to come ride with us in the engineers' cab. In spite of running low on trust during times of no income and health crises, His presence encouraged us to keep puffing and pulling uphill though we could not see around the next bend. At last Norval was called as pastor to a church in a small town of Illinois. Trusting this was what the Lord wanted, we moved in and unpacked. Remembering how the Lord's presence had helped us, we asked Him to stay on with us. Guess we were saying "US and YOU, Lord."[51]

The three-bedroom, parsonage with garage was modern and beautiful. The church members added a large concrete patio for us. Farther out in the back yard a huge mimosa tree spread its branches over our swing, and bloomed for over a month each year filling the air with heavenly fragrance. Beyond that lay farmland as far as the eye could see. We planted fruit trees and had our own vegetable garden. We loved this small town, the people, and our church. Feeling as if we had come home, we thanked God for His bringing us here, and helping us.

All went well for several years, but even seemingly idealistic places are not perfect. The normal ups of church growth, children's accomplishments, and warm fellowship were balanced out by the downs of health problems, financial backsets, and disagreements within the church flock.

We discovered that the goals we had for our children were different from those of their peers. We wanted ours to be God-lovers first of all, and then to do the best they were capable of, looking toward college for each of them. My husband and I prayed together, and separately about these concerns. I remember telling the Lord, *"I do not know what to do, or what You can do, but I am giving You this problem, trusting You for Your best in our family."*

In June 1978, we went to Florida on our very first family vacation, leaving phone numbers where we could be reached in case of emergency. While we were away, some of the church leaders called an illegal business session, stacked the pews with non-attending members, and voted for us to leave. A friend called us so we would know before we returned. We came back early and stayed with close friends in another town to gain perspective. We felt as if we had been slapped, or punished unfairly through underhanded means. Nevertheless, the vote stood, and we were out after four years. They gave us a month's salary, and let us stay in the parsonage a month longer 'til we could find somewhere to move. They never did tell us why they voted us out.

And to think, we had trusted God. *Our train derailed? Where was He? How could He let this happen to us, His children? . . . by His other children?*

Our rejection scale registered a 10. We tried to cope as we packed. The majority of the faithful members were angry and crushed, but helpless as we were to change things. We tried to help our children deal with the whole scene – loss of face, job, housing, friends, and church. Since it was summer, facing those at school was not a problem. Once more we would have to start all over somewhere. They were hurting inside as much as we. This action by church members caused negative seeds about trusting God and believers to be planted deep within them (unbeknownst to us), awaiting a later opportunity to take root in their lives and Christian walk.

We prayed and searched for a place we could afford to rent. Trusting God again, we rented a house in the university town about 25 miles away, and moved ourselves. Our son and daughters started new schools and made new friends whose goals and home training were similar to ours.

After seeking the Lord about work, my husband found a quality control job in a local factory. A church we had visited offered me a part-time secretary's job that made up for the loss of income from piano lessons.

We all attended a local church until my husband accepted a small pastorate about 60 miles away. He drove up each Sunday morning and returned that night, so our family would not be uprooted again. Our teenagers participated in choirs, puppetry, missions, and ministries at the local church. They were relieved that they were no longer the p.k's (preacher's kids) at the church where their dad was pastor. However, our whole family went with Norval for holidays and special programs to his out-of-town pastorate.

This was our lifestyle for the next eight years until our youngest finished high school. Our family members clung to each other as our home train lurched and swayed over the difficult, rugged route of learning more about trusting Him. The Lord was engineering the whole time, and knew exactly what was best for our family. He answered our prayers – by moving us!

Norval and I sought God's forgiveness for thinking we only needed His input, rather than allowing Him to reign in everything. In turn, we were able to forgive the offending church members, and in time forget the heartache of those days. Healing began for us when 37 of the small town church members surprised us on my birthday in the fall by coming to our home with food and all the trimmings. Each year after that a small group came and celebrated my birthday as long as we were in Illinois.

After our third teen graduated from high school, we moved again – this time to South Carolina. My husband had kept his promise to the family, and God had kept His to us, faithfully keeping our train on track.

We had always believed the Lord should be first; learning how to let Him was the hard part. Norval and I emerged from this bittersweet experience, humbly trusting in "Jehovah-Rohi," our Shepherd. "The Lord is my Shepherd; I shall not want"[52] took up permanent residence in our hearts and lives. The Lord had moved us spiritually from "US and GOD"[53] to "GOD and US,"[54] which was a milestone of growth in our learning to trust Him, but not the end of our journey.

SCRIPTURES and NOTES

48 Psalm 103:12
As far as the east is from the west, so far has He removed our transgressions from us.

49 John 10:11, 14
I am the good shepherd. The good shepherd gives His life for the sheep.
I am the good shepherd; and I know My sheep, and am known by My own.

50 Luke 15:4-5, 7
What man of you, having a hundred sheep, if he loses one of them, does not leave the ninety-nine in the wilderness, and go after the one which is lost until he finds it?
And when he has found it, he lays it on his shoulders, rejoicing.
I say to you that likewise there will be more joy in heaven over one sinner who repents than over ninety-nine just persons who need no repentance.

51 Watchman Nee, Song of Songs, (Fort Washington, Pennsylvania: Christian Literature Crusade, 1965), p. 94.

52 Psalm 23:1

53 Watchman Nee, Song of Songs, (Fort Washington, Pennsylvania: Christian Literature Crusade, 1965), p. 94.

54 Watchman Nee, Song of Songs, (Fort Washington, Pennsylvania: Christian Literature Crusade, 1965), p. 139.

EMERALD
The Color of Healing

Emerald green is the color of life and eternal spring. It speaks of beauty and growth and health. Emerald green represents not just life, but life forever where the rainbow around God's throne resembles an emerald.[55] This distinctive shade of green ranges from bright to darker, depending on its natural formation.

Green, a never-tiring color, is produced when yellow and blue are mixed, the way God's never-tiring Power is seen when His light and truth are combined. Emerald green seems the perfect color to express the eternal, healing power of the Lord God Almighty that is operative today.

Though I have already mentioned my early trachs, I will recap here as background for this story. At age two I came down with diphtheria and pneumonia requiring an emergency tracheostomy. With a trach one breathes through the short metal tube inserted in the windpipe below the voice box. The process was repeated when I was five due to measles. Though both trachs were only needed for a few weeks, the panic of not being able to breathe was permanently lodged within and associated with trachs. So was the horror of not being able to talk. Through years of hoarseness and frequent throat infections as I grew up, I continually dreaded the possibility of a third trach.

My double-scarred trachea gradually thickened over the years. In my 40's, my breathing passage was only 40 percent open, making surgery no longer an option. If this surgery were successful, trachs and the fear of them would belong only in my past.

In the spring of 1977, I read somewhere that we give to God what we feel is "worthwhile" such as our talents, our time, and our money, but we tolerate and keep our "worthless" areas such as failures, inadequacies, and handicaps. Right then I gave to God my "bad throat" to do with as He pleased. Realizing with sudden awareness that my throat was not my only "bad" area, I gave God all the incomplete, scarred, and dwarfed areas I knew. I found it hard to praise Him for these "bad" areas, but I did.

Now God was free to work, and He set His plan in motion.

In March after a frightening, choking spell, my doctor sent me to Barnes Hospital in St. Louis to Dr. Stanley Thawley. He was a throat specialist who just happened to be a Christian! Surgery to replace my scarred trachea was recommended and scheduled for June. This surgery would require my wearing a trach for six weeks.

In May, as I read *THE GIFT OF INNER HEALING,*[56] I learned that unseen emotional scars from preschool surgeries many times are more devastating than visible scars. It was possible that my feelings remembered the early fears, anger, and anxiety, whereas my mind had closed them out. Just in case this were true, I asked the Lord to bring the hidden hurts to light, and to heal those buried wounds as He saw fit.

In June 1977, surgery came and went. My voice went also, since air could no longer pass through my voice box. I left the hospital after a few days, weak and with the "dreaded trach." Those next six weeks were difficult. Returning home with an Eversharp pencil and yellow notepads, I faced the inevitable. I had to write all comments whether they were silly or serious. I scribbled directions for household chores. I explained on paper to my impatient children why they could not go somewhere. Our nine-year-old accidentally called my Eversharp the "everlasting pencil" one day. The name stuck – maybe because it was "eternally" used!

Besides filling stacks of notepads attesting to the difficulty of writing everything during these days, coughing spells were frequent and weakness lingered. When alone, there was no way I could answer a ringing phone, so I just stared at it in utter helplessness. With a trach, my sense of smell was gone. I showered keeping the water below my neck, and sang not at all! Being forgetful and buttoning a blouse all the way up cut off my air! Terri, my toy fox terrier, just stared in bewilderment when I opened the back door and snapped my fingers for her to go out or come in, instead of talking to her. On most days I felt like the proverbial frog who jumped up three feet and slid back two, trying to get out of the well. I kept telling myself, "This misery is worth it all, for soon I will have breathing and talking freedom."

The six weeks finally passed and we returned to Barnes. Dr. Thawley knew how fearful I was when they put me to sleep, so each time he held my hand and talked to me until I was out. This time after checking my throat, Dr. Thawley said, "You are going to need to wear your trach for SIX MONTHS."

"What happened to six weeks?" I wrote in apprehension on a yellow notepad. He explained that the rebuilt trachea of grafted skin and bone slivers needed more time to heal undisturbed.

"I have lived with hoarseness and whispering," I later scrawled to my husband, "but six months of writing everything down is unthinkable!"

Nevertheless, I returned home to face the grim task of non-verbal communication. The inability to speak pushed me beyond words to seek other ways to "talk." Eye contact became essential. Eyes rivet attention, laugh, rebuke, tease, love, and cloud with empathy. Eyes as varied in colors as an autumn sunset reveal the emotions of the soul, wordlessly and instantly. If eye contact were missing, I found that by touching others lightly, I had their immediate attention.

Listening also moved from black-and-white to color. Without my voice to interrupt, my full attention was available to others as they talked. These communication tools of seeing and hearing with my heart became almost as priceless as spoken words, yet they came at a high cost to me.

In the fourth month of the six-month waiting period, I

came down with severe throat pain and a high fever, necessitating a return to Dr. Thawley. After more surgery, he explained, "I had to remove the surgical props holding your reconstructed windpipe in place because the whole area was infected."

I scribbled in haste, "When infection is gone, what is next?"

"Nothing more can be done. This surgery was our last option. You will wear a trach for life," my doctor said, slowly shaking his head. "The throat surgery we had such hopes for has failed."

Shock waves of realization ricocheted within. I had been ready to talk normally after surgery, or prepared to die during surgery, but not to wear a trach for life. The impossible had happened. I WOULD WEAR A TRACH AS LONG AS I LIVED!

Despair rolled in like a winter fog that shrouds its surroundings. Not really caring about much, I watched one afternoon as the other bed in my room was rolled out and a crib wheeled in. A nurse explained that my new roommate was a two-year-old girl with a new trach because of severe bronchitis. Amy was a curly-haired blond just as I had been at that age. The next morning I watched Amy play and soundlessly "read" her books. For a long time she stood at the side of her crib. When big silent tears appeared and dropped on the edge of her mattress, I knew Amy was crying. Unable to comfort her with my voice, I got up and went over to her tall crib. Reaching up through the bars, I put my arms snugly around her and held her. Amy was consoled.

In return, her small hand reached over the crib's edge and patted the top of my head. A deep sadness overwhelmed me as I thought of someone her size left with bewildering voicelessness, loneliness, pain, and fear. I hurt for Amy, for myself, and for the two-year-old child still trapped within me.

Time stood still as the eternity-filled voice of God resounded within, "I planned Amy's being here in your room, so you could see what it was like for you." My heart cried out to

God as He revealed this hidden hurt, still sore after all these years. As I stood there in the light of His presence, the heavy sadness within about my early experiences left, and peace came. Inner healing had begun.

I wondered, *Is outer healing possible, too?*

Returning to my bed, I was momentarily aglow because of God's touch and Amy's. Touching communicated. Touching satisfied. A hug had silently said to Amy, "I care." Holding hands later that day with my husband told me, "You are still special." Norval's arm around my shoulder or waist spoke of strength and support as he spent time with me. I could not recall a time when he had ever been embarrassed by my throat problems or my trach, just sympathetic. A friend's hand resting on my arm warmly communicated love and concern. Touching was not vocal, yet it spoke volumes.

Desperately trying to stop the unraveling of my life, I sought security in working the jigsaw puzzles at the hospital. They provided a place where everything fit together and held. I could depend on them to tongue-and-groove until the picture was complete. Dr. Thawley came to my hospital room one day when I was dejectedly uniting shapes and colors. I wrote, *"I can make the pieces of this puzzle fit, but what about my life? None of the pieces fit anymore. What am I going to do?"*

Dr. Thawley countered by saying, "Wearing a trach is not the worst thing that could have happened to you. You still have options. I suggest that you get an artificial larynx since your vocal chords are fine."

My husband bought a used one for me immediately. Holding the battery-operated beige unit to my neck only increased my dilemma. One minute I was thrilled because it would allow me to leave the prison of silence. The next minute I hated it because I sounded like a robot. In this emotional stalemate, I was too upset and too embarrassed to even practice using it in the hospital.

I discarded my throat infection at the hospital, but brought home smoldering resentment over needing a lifetime trach. I no longer wanted to commune even silently with the God who directs all things, for I felt He had let me down.

As I reluctantly began "mechanically talking," I discovered that using the artificial larynx was easier than writing everything down. Our 14-year-old son said in a teasing mood one day, "If you don't talk to me using your right voice, I am going to Jim's where his mother will." I promptly made a face at him and waved him out of the room. Once in a shoe store with my family, I expressed an opinion using my beige "voicer." Our soon-to-be-teenage daughter came to where I was and whispered, "Mom, don't use that in here. Everyone is looking."

Books and articles on healing seemed to gravitate toward me. Hoping the experiences of others might recharge my faith battery, I read books by Agnes Sanford,[57] Oral Roberts,[58] and Kathryn Kuhlman.[59] The Guideposts[60] magazine arrived monthly offering me much needed inspiration.

Christian friends encouraged me to dwell on scriptures about healing. I was urged to thank God for healing my throat every time I felt pain when I turned my head too far, or had to clean out the always-messy trach. Radical advice for one who felt short-circuited by God, but I needed to hear it. My favorite verse became "O Lord my God, I cried out to You, and You have healed me."[61]

Over the months prayers and verses about healing finally penetrated my defenses, allowing the anger and anguish to seep out like a slow leak in a tire. A lonesomeness within my soul emerged. Fellowship with the Lord was becoming more important than what I wanted Him to do. At last I prayed not with great fanfare but with a broken spirit saying,

> *God, I resign as 'lord' of my throat. Forgive me for blaming You. I would like to be rid of this trach, but I will rejoice in You daily and praise You as long as I live, in spite of the discomfort and inconvenience of this trach. I offer You myself, trach and all.*

About eight months after surgery, I began to feel cool air

in my throat as I breathed. Experimenting one day I placed my finger over the trach hole, forced the air up through my own vocal cords, and found I could speak again! To say I was ecstatic understates the moment. As my desire to speak again became reality, I covered the trach hole and praised the Lord with my VOICE! Then I called Dr. Thawley long distance using my own voice, and his excitement almost matched mine. He asked, "How soon can you get to St. Louis? I must see your throat at once." Talking with the trach hole covered was definitely better than sounding like a robot.

When Dr. Thawley examined me the next day, he was surprised and elated, telling us, "Body tissues are set within six months of surgery, so I expected you to use the artificial larynx for the rest of your life. I have felt bad that your surgery did not go as planned. I hated for you to have to wear a trach for the rest of your life. But, I am so happy that you can now use your own voice with the trach."

As I sewed new clothes, I made matching neckbands that attached to the sides of my sterling-silver trach, allowing it to sometimes pass as jewelry. In May I dreamed of the window of heaven again, only this time it was rounded. The music and light pouring out surrounded me. In November I was hired as a part-time church secretary talking readily with my "fingered trach." I was learning that living with a trach as a friend is easier than as a foe!

One day I remember correcting my daughter in our hallway about a forgotten chore when she said, "Mom, you are shouting at me." Trach-talking was weak at best, so I was incredulous and responded, "You know I cannot shout with a trach."

She came back with, "It is not the loudness, it's the intensity."

Every three or four months over a period of four years I returned for check-ups. Mystified, Dr. Thawley checked my throat, saying things like, "Your throat looks different," or "Somehow it has changed from last time."

The Lord's resources are as unlimited as they are unfathomable. After three-and-a-half years of trach-talking, the Lord used the healing touch of a Christian chiropractor as part of the healing process. Dr. Donald Odum realigned my weakened bones and muscles. He prayed as he pressed the God-given points on my body to restore life-flowing energy especially to my throat. Soon my throat felt alive again, warm and moist.

Finally after four long years, we heard Dr. Thawley say those unbelievably beautiful words, "Your trach is no longer needed because your trachea is now 80 percent open. With amazement in his voice, he said, "I've never seen this happen before, or even heard of it happening. I'm so happy for you."

Besides sustaining me when my lines of communication were down, the Great Physician planned more for me than just breathing and talking freedom. Wholeness involved His Lordship; instead of my schedule of six weeks, it took four years of physical pain and spiritual struggle. Orchestrating it all, the Lord was lovingly and miraculously healing inner and outer hurts. Psalm 30:2 was true, "O Lord my God, I cried out to You, and You have healed me." When the Lord healed my throat, He also healed my propensity for throat infections and hoarseness. Since 1981 these are so rare they are practically nonexistent.

The Lord's light shining on the truth of His Word produced the power within me to effect the healing of my throat. Green, signifying life and growth, has become for me the emerald green of abundant life and health. The eternal, healing power of "Jehovah-Rophe" (I AM the Lord who heals you)[62] is as awesome today as in Bible times.

SCRIPTURES and NOTES

55 Revelation 4:3

And He who sat there was like a jasper and a sardius stone in appearance; and there was a rainbow around the throne, in appearance like an emerald.

56 Jean Carter Stapleton, THE GIFT OF INNER HEALING, (Waco, Texas: Word Publishing Co.), 1976.

57 Agnes Mary White Sanford, THE HEALING LIGHT, (New York, New York: Ballantine Publishing Group), revised 1972.

58 Oral Roberts, THE MIRACLE BOOK, (Tulsa, Oklahoma: Pinoak Publications), 1972

59 Kathryn Kuhlman, GOD CAN DO IT AGAIN, (Englewood Cliffs, New Jersey: Prentice-Hall, Inc., Guideposts Edition), 1969

60 Guideposts Associates, "GUIDEPOSTS," (Carmel, New York: Guideposts Associates, Inc.).

61 Psalm 30:2

62 Exodus 15:26

And (Moses quoting the Lord) said, If you diliently heed the voice of the Lord your God and do what is right in His sight, give ear to His commandments and keep all His statutes, I will put none of the diseases on you which I have brought on the Egyptians. For I am the Lord who heals you.

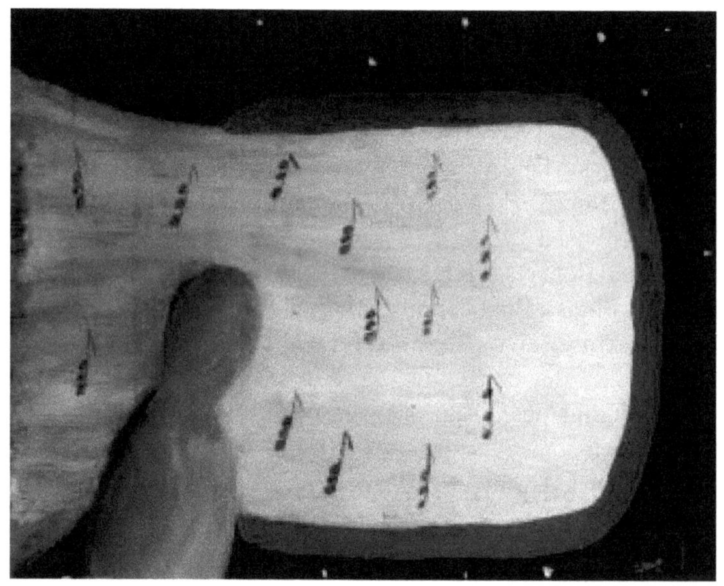

SECOND VIEW OF HEAVEN

When I saw the windows of heaven this time, several things were different. The windows were rounded, and I could not tell how they opened. The harmonious, lilting, compelling, beautiful music and ethereal light flowed out freely toward me, surrounding me with the glories of heaven.

I still do not know why the window changed. I can only hope that during the intervening 36 years between the two window visions that I have grown spiritually, and therefore perceive the windows of heaven differently. At the very least I see myself in this one, whereas I was not in the first. This time the music and light poured out the window and surrounded me, possibly meaning I am now involved in heavenly as well as earthly things.

CRANBERRY
The Color Of Helping

Cranberries are a deep, rich red. In the fall, trees and leaves turn a deep autumnal red, a perfect choice for sweaters and scarves. Cranberry-colored clothing speaks of dignity and depth, yet warmth. Redbrick buildings in the cranberry shade give the effect of being stately without being austere.

Going from violet of one rainbow into red of the next one, we come to a berry shade of red, still being influenced by the bluish tones of the first rainbow. In "color talk" this means it does not take much truth (blue) to deepen love (red). The truth as stated by King David, "God is my helper,"[63] gives the added dimension of His direct involvement as part of His love.

Norval and I were learning to live in the "CHRIST and US"[64] mode. We now sought the Lord first in decisions and daily living, and never more so than at the college-choice time for our firstborn.

Norval Lee Bard, Jr., was starting his junior year in public high school when we began to seriously think about his college selection. He was an above-average student who enjoyed languages and history, and whose five close high school friends were likewise achievers, competitive, and college-bent. They enjoyed games of all kinds in each other's homes, and watched sports together on TV. For fun and exercise they played basketball on the driveways, and rode bikes. They were a close-knit group who planned to go away to school together. The college decision seemed settled, . . . almost.

My husband and I had come from different educational backgrounds. He had a degree from a state school and I had graduated from a Christian college. We agreed that the knowledge gained was similar, but the approach was entirely different. The professors and leaders at the Christian school had offered individual help. By being available at school and home to talk and pray about problems or concerns, they helped their students succeed. Their inherent reaffirmation of "Judeo-Christian" values tipped the scales toward Christian schools, in our opinion.

In addition, we had prayed daily for our children from the time we knew they were on the way. We wanted them to become "God lovers" first and foremost. We committed their choices of friends, colleges, marriage partners, careers, and goals to the Lord and His perfect plan for each one. In light of their spiritual growth, we decided that for our family evangelical colleges would best continue the college-agers' Christian development. However, the choice of which Christian school would be left up to each of our children.

This time had come for our firstborn. One fall day with more bravado than I felt, I faced the inevitable by saying, "College days will be here before you know it. We need to be making definite plans for 'the Philistines are upon you.'[65] When can your dad and I begin talking with you about this?"

"How about tonight after supper?" he said.

We three met and soon discovered as we pooled our ignorance that we had no facts about schools, financial aid, or requirements. Our son offered to see his high school counselor. We planned to check out resources at the library. We also wanted to talk with other parents who had traveled this college-decision road.

"Let's meet again next week, and remember to pray about this," his dad suggested.

Since the right to choose is God-given, choices are always available, inevitable, and consequential. Because we parents wanted to help our son make the right college choice for him, we prayed something like this:

> *Lord, we are committed to You and Your purposes for us and for this wonderful son You have loaned us. Do not let us blow what You might be doing. We need Your guidance to make the right choice, and ask You to provide the finances to make it possible. Grant us wisdom*

and courage and anything else we will need. In Jesus' name, Amen.

We read a variety of materials covering everything from college selection to parental guidance at this time. We did seek advice from Christian friends, hearing both positive and negative results.

At our next family conference, information flowed. Norval Lee started out by saying, "Because of grants, loans and financial aid, my counselor said it would be advantageous for me to choose a school in our state."

"That would also cut down on transportation costs for you and us," his dad added.

Finding it hard to even think about his leaving, I found this idea very appealing, so grinning sheepishly, I added, "Sounds good to me."

Our son went on, "The costs vary as much as $4,000.00 between state and private schools because the state schools are federally funded. Since I'm going to need financial help, a state school is the logical choice."

His dad responded, "We believe your first experience living away from home should be within Christian surroundings, in spite of the cost. We covet for you the right to be led and taught by professionals who not only fear God and walk with Him daily, but are free to communicate this to their students. I wish I had experienced this long before seminary. Your faith will undergo times of close scrutiny and doubts, yet in a Godly environment faith could emerge strengthened – not slaughtered. While I was at a state school and in the army, I saw devastating things happen to those who were away from home for the first time."

"Well," Norval Lee retorted, "those 'devastating things' happen on Christian campuses too, don't they?"

"Absolutely. There are no guarantees," I admitted. "But an evangelical campus is covered with prayer for the staff, students, and faculty continually. We have been praying about your college choice since before you were born, wanting only God's best for you."

"And," I continued, "if you should fall in love during college days, your opportunities for marrying a believer and having a Godly home would be tremendously increased by living on a Christian campus."

"I think getting a practical degree in political science would be hampered by a Christian education," our son contended. "If I graduate with a narrow, lop-sided education, what about job placement? To graduate from a university that is prominent in my field could be a real asset, not to mention getting to know outstanding people in my field. Seems like you all are closing your minds to what some state schools have to offer. Furthermore, how do you know that God does not want me at a state university?"

"We don't," I had to admit, "but we do know that since God is in control of everything, we can trust Him to lead us now.

"We seem to have reached an impasse tonight," his dad concluded, "but let's meet again next week, and let's keep on praying and seeking."

The next week we narrowed the college choices together. Elimination of schools for one reason or another progressed until there were just two left: Wheaton College and University of Illinois. The pull of wanting to be with his friends was strong: not wanting to discount his parents' conviction was equally strong.

Norval Lee could have chosen to insist, "I am old enough to make my own decisions, so I am going with my friends." Or he could have rebelled and said, "Forget college, if it is going to be such a hassle!" He did neither.

We could have chosen to decree with all the parental authority we could muster, "You are not going to a state school!" Or we could have taken the easy route and said, "Your college choice is totally up to you." We did neither.

Norval Lee brought home the entrance data for both colleges from his school counselor, and added, "Wheaton is ranked among the best evangelical colleges in our nation. Because a very large number of freshmen request admission each year, this school has to reject over half the applications, regardless of student achievement, personality, and location. I guess my chances of going there are about nil."

Suddenly an inspired thought descended, winging its way straight to my heart. With hope and apprehension, I suggested, "How about a compromise, Son?"

"What do you mean?" he asked cautiously.

"If the Christian school selects you, you go there as a first choice. If it refuses you, you are free to go to the state school," I ventured.

Feeling he would probably not be accepted by the first choice, and maybe out of deference to us, he said, "That's okay by me!" With that, he applied for admission to both schools. He felt safe with this agreement, for it almost assured him that he would be with his friends in the fall.

After these discussions, we still believed the Christian-college decision we made years ago was the right choice for our children. Now our conviction stood face to face with reality; the outcome unknown.

My husband and I fervently prayed,

> *Lord, we have done all we can do. The rest is up to You. You know the future, and You know our son's heart. He is Yours by his choice. You are in control of his life. If possible, we ask that he be admitted to the Christian school. Realizing You are not limited to a certain place, Lord, Your will be done in this. In Jesus' name, Amen.*

As part of summer vacation our family visited both schools. Father and son returned to Wheaton College in October for a private interview required of all applicants. We wondered what our son said to the counselor, but did not pry.

In November of his senior year, Norval Lee was accepted at the University of Illinois, and given a room assignment with one of his friends.

The weeks dragged by as we anxiously waited to hear from the evangelical school. At last, in February of his senior year, a letter arrived from Wheaton College.

As Norval Lee eagerly opened it, his face revealed a sequence of emotions – tenseness, surprise, astonishment, incredulity. Then he read aloud, "We are happy to inform you that you have been accepted . . ." His only comment was, "I wonder why they chose me – but I like being chosen."

How the Lord pulled off that miracle, we will never know. My husband and I thanked the Lord over and over for this Christian school, and for our son's becoming a part of it. We are likewise grateful for the scholarships, work-ships and loans.

The Christian college experience there caused his faith to mature. He found committed believers among his new peers. The spiritual depth of his professors profoundly influenced his growth. He graduated with purpose and plans. He appreciated his Christian heritage. He now desired to please his Lord with his life.

What we did not know until five years after he had finished college was that Norval Lee had also chosen to pray when he was accepted at the Christian school, telling the Lord,

> *This is it. If I do not find Christians there who live what they believe, I am ready to chuck this whole Christian business. I have seen enough hypocrisy to last me a lifetime.*

What a miracle indeed! We parents did not know how critical this college decision really was to his spiritual health. But, God did, and He worked all things together for the good of all.

The redbrick buildings of Wheaton College are stately without being austere, indicative of the dignity and depth and warmth found within. Our loving Lord, who led Jonathan Blanchard in 1860 to start Wheaton College, knew that our son would need to be there one day. Then He made it possible. The Lord's direct involvement as part of His love bore out the truth "God is my (our) helper."[66]

SCRIPTURES and NOTES

63 Psalm 54:4
Behold, God is my helper; the Lord is with those who uphold my life.

64 Watchman Nee, Song of Songs, (Fort Washington, Pennsylvania: Christian Literature Crusade, 1965), p. 139.

65 Judges 16:12
Therefore Delilah took new ropes and bound him with them, and said to him, The Philistines are upon you, Samson! And men were lying in wait, staying in the room. But he broke them off his arms like a thread.

66 Psalm 54:4

STEEL BLUE
The Color Of Security

Steel blue is a metallic shade that symbolizes strength. Steel is an alloy of iron and carbon produced by extreme heat. It becomes a solid component and support when used in buildings, heavy equipment, machinery, train rails, and vehicles. Though not indestructible, with normal use it is very strong and unbending.

Blue symbolizes truth. Steel blue suggests the added qualities of being strong and unchanging. Truth is strong because it does not change. The Lord is truth,[67] and His commanding presence is strong and unchanging. He said to Moses, "I AM WHO I AM" (Jehovah),[68] and to Malachi, "For I AM the Lord, I do not change."[69]

Change is inevitable on earth, but it is not welcomed at any age. It threatens security, for it goes against the grain of what is. That is why the only changes I felt safe with were inner ones. Though sincere, I unwittingly prayed in the fall of 1985,

> *Change me inside, Lord. Make me more like You. Teach me how to better relate to others, even if You have to drag me kicking and screaming all the way.*

I promptly forgot all about this dramatic prayer as our lives moved into the fast-spin cycle of Thanksgiving and Christmas, but the Lord did not . . .

After the holidays our security started its downward descent when my husband, Norval, came from work saying, "I'm being laid off. My boss told me that because business is so slow, tomorrow is my last day for a while."

Change paraded into the center stage of my thinking, costumed in disbelief and trembling with fear. Job security? Not any more! My tumbling thoughts halted when I looked up and saw Norval just standing there. Going over to hug him I asked, "Did they say for how long?"

"No, it all depends on the economy," he sighed.

A devastating financial storm was surely headed our way. Already gale-force winds of house and car payments, plus our children's education tore at our budget. Our son, Norval Lee, was doing graduate work in France; our older daughter, Shannon, was a junior at Baptist College, Charleston, South Carolina, and Heather, our high-school girl graduating in June, planned to start ORU in Tulsa in the fall. My part-time secretarial job for a local business covered our needs about like a paper parasol in a downpour.

We updated Norval's resume and sent out scores of copies. Classified ads became required daily reading. He applied everywhere for any kind of job, but heard nothing. Looming over us was the awareness that unemployment checks were only for six months. What then? We were driven to pray more often, just to cope. On the practical side we cut expenses to the bone, had yard sales, and contacted our creditors about making smaller payments.

After three hopeless months, it became obvious we must sell our beloved house. When the "FOR SALE" sign was planted in our front lawn, we admitted, "If God does not sell the house by the time the unemployment checks run out, we are sunk." The security we had felt within our four walls boomeranged into nightmares. Trying to imagine no house, no income, and no food was beyond us, so we clung to the hope that the next 90 days were surely time enough for the Lord to send a buyer.

Then our college daughter in Charleston called her dad with a suggestion so unexpected that its possibility captivated us. "Why don't you come here and look for work?"

"Are they hiring there? Even a man past 50?" he had inquired hopefully.

"You've got nothing to lose," she continued, "and who

knows, maybe a job to gain. There is industry here, and civilian jobs connected with the military, and construction is going on . . . anyway it is worth a try."

"We will pray about it and seriously consider it," he commented. Setting down the phone he reflected aloud, "I guess one state is as good as another to hunt for work." Within a few days he was driving southeast. When our son arrived from France in mid-May, he joined his dad in Charleston, looking for work.

Talk about change, for the first time in our marriage of nearly 30 years Norval and I were living apart, each of us operating as single parents. In countdown for Heather's high school graduation, she and I attended school luncheons and honor's banquets, while her dad, brother, and sister in Charleston hunted jobs and apartments. They returned to Illinois for Heather's graduation in June. Since she was seeking summer work, she chose to go with the others back to Charleston. This left me (and my toy fox terrier, Jeremy) to sell the house, pack up, and move down.

Bills kept coming in. Phone calls between Norval and me increased our indebtedness, but we needed the encouragement of talking to each other. When not at work, I kept packing, as my ever-running monologue spiraled upward,

Lord, we need jobs . . . Send a buyer for the house . . .
Put our family together soon . . . You know I love you. . .
I am trying hard not to worry,[70] *but this is serious!*

Gray-faced skies began to smile the day a buyer named Paul said he would buy our house at the end of July. Things looked brighter still when Heather was placed in summer mission work. Then Norval found a manufacturing job. Our son went to work for a landscaping company. They were able to rent an apartment in July for our family.

At last, Lord," I said aloud, *"It looks like things are working out. Thanks for helping us."* I resigned from work as of Monday, July 28, and engaged movers for July 30.

My life strings were stretched to their limits, I thought, until July 23 when I found a yellow delivery notice of a registered letter in the mail. Taking time from packing to hurry back across town, I traded the yellow slip for a white envelope at the post office. I tore it open with apprehension and read,

> Due to circumstances beyond my control, I cannot carry through with buying your house as planned. I am sorry for having to back out at this late date, and for not getting to enjoy your house.
>
> Sincerely, Paul

Panic stricken, I cried aloud in frustration, *"Not a 'NO,' Lord. Not now! The moving van will be here a week from today."* Now I went into crisis praying.

> *Lord, unless You do something this week, we are wiped out. There is no way we can afford both this house and an apartment. No house sale means no money for movers. I cannot even think about what You might be able to change at this late date!*

Change had ceased to be my enemy.

Depression got up with me the next morning (July 24) and followed me to work, dragging at my heels. My boss took one look at me and asked, "Are you okay?"

"No," I said, "our house sale fell through, and I do not know what to do. We cannot move, but I cannot afford to stay here. I do not want to cancel the movers, . . .but I better not quit work either. Anyway, thanks for asking," I added through trembling lips as I turned to my desk.

"Wait a minute," he said, "what is your house like? What is your selling price? How much do you owe? Is it listed with a realtor?"

Thinking he might put me in touch with a buyer, I freely answered all his questions. I added, "The difference between our asking price and what we owe goes to pay the movers." Returning to my desk, I found it difficult to keep my agitated mind geared to the work at hand.

That long weekend I literally prayed without ceasing.

> *Lord, we can do nothing to help ourselves. We are as helpless as the Israelites were, trapped at the Red Sea with the Egyptians in hot pursuit. You knew just what to do for them, and You are in charge here, too. . . Show us the way out, or through.*

I was tempted to give up as my hope was ragged. My ability to cope was unraveling fast. Yet something about stepping out in faith, even if it meant walking in the dark, struggled to surface. I forced myself to continue packing so I would be ready. For what? I did not know. Maybe I was putting feet to my prayers, or maybe just keeping busy doing the only thing I knew to do.

On Monday I went in to work wondering if this were to be my last day there or not. My boss immediately called me into his office. "Has anything changed for you over the weekend?"

"No," I replied curiously.

"I have decided to buy your house as an investment for rental property," he went on. "You are asking a fair price. I do not want to pass it up. My lawyer is waiting to start processing the sale as soon as he gets the necessary papers. Can you get them to him now?"

"How long will it take him?" I asked in a daze.

"He hopes to have some documents ready for us to sign tomorrow. He will finalize the paper work later and send it to you by mail. Is the moving van still coming on Wednesday?"

By this time I had recovered enough to answer, "Yes." I tried to thank him, but he waved me on, saying, "Three months is long enough to be away from your family. Now go get those papers."

My inner depression somersaulted into frenzied excitement as I bolted across the parking lot. I "hallelujah-ed" all the way home in my car. I praised the Lord loudly using every name for Him I knew. Change can be good, I decided.

Arriving home, I grabbed the phone, gushing in ecstasy to my family what God had done through my boss. With grateful hearts, we all rejoiced to be "movin' on." Then off to the lawyer, and back to work to finish secretarial things, . . . and say good-bye.

I did not remember the part of my prayer about learning to better relate to others, but God did . . .

I slept fitfully Monday night, aware that I had to cram into the next day what would normally take a week. Errands to the lawyer, bank, pharmacy, Phone Company, and utilities would take the whole day. But I also needed to be home to finish packing before the van arrived early the next morning.

On Tuesday morning I sent an urgent plea heavenward,

> *Lord, I need to be twins today. I have neither time nor energy to do the errands and packing, too. Would you send someone to help me?*

Before I finished eating breakfast an acquaintance from church called. Evlyn Jones and I rarely talked by phone. She had never been to my home. She said, "I heard you are moving this week. Could you use some help? I am free to come today, if you need me."

Hanging up the phone, I stood amazed, so overwhelmed I was barely able to mutter, *"Thanks, Lord."*

Evlyn came bringing a fresh fruit salad for our lunch. She stayed at our house, and conquered those last-minute chores like a veteran while I ran errands. She put the furniture to be sold in the front yard and sold it! She defrosted and cleaned out the refrigerator, packed the rest of my kitchen stuff, and labeled it. She swept, vacuumed, and took phone messages. I was humbled by her ministry of love as she tackled those menial chores for me. When I tried to thank her, she said, "Just doing what needs to be done – maybe not like you would do it – but I trust it is all right." It was more than all right, for her ministry showed me how to relate better by lovingly serving others in need.

Wednesday, July 30 dawned bright and clear. The moving van came, loaded up, and left. Our barren house now stood as a silent sentinel to the steel-blue fact that the Lord is in control of *WHAT* happens to us, as well as *WHEN* it happens. Change is a formidable weapon in His hand. As my canine companion, Jeremy, and I headed for South Carolina, I went on my way rejoicing that our security is in the Lord Who changes not, but Who can change all things.[71] He relentlessly moves us on to greater trust in spite of our kicking and screaming all the way.

SCRIPTURES and NOTES

67 John 14:6

Jesus said to him, I am the way, the truth, and the life. No one comes to the Father except through Me.

68 Exodus 3:14

And God said to Moses, I AM WHO I AM. And He said, Thus you shall say to the children of Israel, I AM has sent me to you.

69 Malachi 3:6

For I AM the Lord, I do not change; therefore you are not consumed, O sons of Jacob.

70 Matthew 6:33-34

But seek first the kingdom of God and His righteousness, and all these things shall be added to you. Therefore do not worry about tomorrow, for tomorrow will worry about its own things. Sufficient for the day is its own trouble.

71 Psalm 50:15

Call on Me in the day of trouble; I will deliver you and you shall glorify me.

AZURE
The Color of Peace

What color would you say peace is?

I conducted a non-scientific poll among friends and relatives. Each one without fail, after a few moments, said, "Peace is blue like the sky." This color is commonly called azure.

Azure is blue that has been lightened. When the blue of truth is illuminated with the pure light of our Lord, His peace flows. Since blue is the spiritual color, it is not only possible but probable that peace, being an attribute of God, would be azure.

God-given peace is mentioned frequently in the Bible. Isaiah called the Lord "the Prince of Peace."[72] After God said to Gideon, "Peace be with you," Gideon built an altar to the Lord and called it "Jehovah-Shalom," The-Lord-Is-Peace.[73] "Shalom"[74] is used as a greeting in the Mideast. It means peace, but conveys more than peace – namely blessings and wholeness. Peace is the assurance that trust in the Lord is adequate, no matter what storms rage. In order to learn about peace under pressure, it becomes necessary for us to tread the pressure mill of life.

As I grew up, I learned that achievement meant acceptance. Handicaps were not to be deterrents. After years of trying, my achievements never seemed enough to fill the void inside me. My life-long walk with God was special, but I was still not satisfied. I had striven in my own strength to fill the roles of daughter, sister, student, teacher, secretary, wife, mother, and now, grandmother.

Misunderstandings in 1993 between my siblings and me resulted in unexpected harsh words, left unresolved. Crying did not relieve my distress. I began having erratic stomach pains that felt like the ulcer I had more than 30 years before. I started taking soothing stomach medicine when the pains came.

Then my octogenarian mother was struck by a car in November of 1993 as she walked to vote. She spent the next two months between CICU and a nursing home. I flew to Kentucky to spend a week with her twice during her hospital stay. Norval and I drove up to be with her at the nursing home during Christmas. Flying put tremendous pressure on our strained budget, whereas car trips did the same to our bodies.

On New Year's Day 1994 (according to my prayer journal) I prayed, *"Change anything in me that is blocking You or Your will."* I never once thought about how He might do it, but I was to find out.

My mother died January 12, 1994, adding grief to my already stressed-out emotions. I returned from her funeral more tired than I could ever remember. I ate just enough to keep going. Fortified with quick prayers, daily I rushed on, trying to find in my normal activities an antidote to my emptiness and emotional overload.

In April my siblings and I were able to amiably divide Mother's things and empty her house to be sold. I left my inherited things in a storage locker in Louisville. Spring fast-forwarded into summer.

Our friends, Ed and Rita McKinley, offered to loan us their 1975 Dodge van to go to Kentucky to get our stored possessions. The back opened wide enough to load and hold my mother's tall, china closet plus the other things. We made plans to leave on July 8. On July 3 we watched in disbelief as Ed died of a heart attack in the pulpit leading a July 4 program at church. With no emotional reserves, I reacted to his death and our trip dilemma with shooting pains so sharp I bent over and held my stomach each time they came. Increasing the stomach medicine did not help.

Rita called after Ed's funeral and said, "Ed wanted you to use the van, and I still do, so please use it as planned." We left in the van on Friday, attended a college reunion in Kentucky on Saturday, and visited with relatives and friends. As the weekend unfolded, my streaking pains spread and intensified. Weakness caused me to sweat profusely. I rested anywhere I could sit or lie on something.

On Monday Norval and I finished loading the van by noon and started home. Coming through the Smoky Mountains, the van's noisy brakes wore out! Though replacing them took money, time, and energy we did not have, it was not an option.

Two days after we finally returned home, Norval took me to the emergency room with stabbing, throbbing pains around my heart and nearby organs. When I was admitted for observation over the weekend, Norval was relieved to no longer be solely responsible for me. My pulse raced each time a nurse entered the room. I gritted my teeth to endure a difficult IV hookup. Sleeping was reduced to catnaps, for I feared dying in my sleep. Somehow I survived that weekend as the medical staff checked my blood pressure, took blood samples, and did EKGs. On Monday my doctor ordered the heart stress test and the heart rest test. I feared I would die at any moment – not even be able to complete the present test. Having never had any problems with my heart, I imagined the worst.

After several days of testing, the doctors concluded that my heart was fine. Since further testing as an outpatient would suffice, I was sent home with medication to deaden the pain, and pills to help me sleep.

Back in Illinois my friend and prayer partner for over eight years now, Evlyn Jones (mentioned in the last chapter) prayed for me and with me. She called with a message from the Lord for me:

> Enter into this with Me. Like childbirth, we are bringing forth something new. Cooperate with Me through this, for I AM peeling off another layer as you do to an onion. At times it may seem as if you are depending on Me for your very life. You will understand better and see later what is going on. Do not be afraid of what I AM doing; you will survive and be victorious."

I began to despair of how God was going to peel off this layer. Pulling fear to me like a magnet, I grew increasingly uptight. The surges of travail were now accompanied by occasional numbness in legs and arms. Different medications from my doctor produced various complications, but no improvement.

In rare moments of lesser hurting, my computer and I talked to the Lord about everything that was going on. Believing that whatever happens to me has to get by God first,[75] I typed,

> *Is this pain because of something I have done? Did Evlyn hear You right? Are You really just peeling off a layer? I am afraid of my weakness and pain. I shrink from entering into this changing of me – if this is what is happening.*
>
> *I have not wished to die, but I sure think I am going to when the pain surges around my heart. I seem to be at a crossroads where it is a scary step of faith to move on with You, and disastrous to my health if I do not.*

In the quietest voice imaginable way deep down inside me, the Lord said,

> To submit to My request is to stop fighting inside and let go of your ways of responding. AM I enough? AM I able? I AM pleased with where you are, and I AM worthy of your trust.

"Lord," I said, *"would You help me do this by giving me a picture of You to carry me through these rough days?"*

> Immediately I was pulled into a winter scene. The Lord, dressed in dark, shimmering clothing complete with hood, is slowly starting up a hill covered with scattered bushes and shrubs on a dark blue, icy, snowy night. At a snail's pace, He steadily moves forward with His staff in hand.
>
> I am a lone, scraggly, weak sheep whose woolly coat is now yellowed and dirtied by the valley storm.

> Trying to see my Shepherd's feet, I am blinded by the weather. Slowly, step by step, I strain to follow Him by hearing His encouraging voice above the winds.
>
> I understand somehow that He is with me. He is leading, but I must walk through this storm, following Him. This time He cannot carry me by lifting me out of all this, but He is carrying me in a larger sense by loving me into greater trust and victory through it.

Awe-struck, I muttered, *"Thank you, Lord, for hearing me, and help me endure this time of loss."*

It seemed that God was adding to my losses of mother, health, and the hope of a growing bond with my siblings, by removing the layer of trust in Him I had relied on.

Still searching for physical causes, the doctor ordered an upper GI. No problems there. In desperation (I guess), my doctor suggested I talk with qualified counselors just in case my physical pain was rooted in the past, or in stress, or who knows what.

What a blessing in disguise! Christian counselors and I discovered unresolved emotional conflicts carried inside from way back. The deep dark secret within was that I had lived my whole life as a non-person! My emotional development was snagged back in early childhood. Consequently, feelings of inferiority dominated. Step by step I trudged through the molasses of long-ago experiences that held me captive. Awareness. Acceptance. Forgiveness. Releasing. Healing.

Week on unending week I endured this "labor ordeal." I sought scriptures to lean on and talked to God without ceasing, *"Is this a testing time? Spiritual warfare? Am I going to die now, (thinking maybe I had not heard Him correctly earlier)?"*

In His mercy and love, He encouraged me one day at my computer by saying,

> This is not a sickness unto death, but all of this

> is preparation, that I may be glorified in it and through it. You CAN DO this through Me, for I AM strengthening you and know how much you can stand. You are learning love from Me...and trust from Me...and what My truth is.
>
> Quit striving so hard to reach what you think I want you to become during these days. Relax in Me, for I AM with you and I AM leading you. You do not need to seek My approval, for you already have it, along with My love.
>
> I put your emotions in so you would have a release valve for your feelings, but yours have been dammed up, and held captive inside. The physical pain helps break down your defenses, so the hurt can come out. Cry as often as you need to, for you are letting out years of bottled-up hurt. When the pain is no longer needed, it will be gone.

As this message penetrated my protective layers, I allowed tears to come more freely now. But, like a revolving door, I trusted God, then I doubted His methods. I needed Him, then I pulled back. I searched within for causes, then despaired of any growth through pain. I even grew apprehensive lest the Lord decide that changing me was not worth it. I heard myself repeating from time to time, "I can do all things through Christ Who strengthens me."[76]

One day in the midst of these repetitive ruts, the Lord tenderly spoke again,

> I AM worthy of your trust, for I AM trustworthy. We are erasing the out-of-focus trust built into you and replacing it with the trust that comes through My wholeness. Let the little child within you love Me and trust Me. Seek Me until this childlike faith grows and bursts forth from your lifelong cocoon in soaring, in spiritual beauty, and in the new creation of a person filled with joy and vibrant life.

I awakened one morning in August with these words coursing through my mind. I hurriedly grabbed a pencil and wrote:

The little girl of my emotions
Is a joy to behold;
She capers and frolics about,
Longing to be bold.

She hugs the Lord's neck
With a squeeze, and a pat,
And says, "I love You, You know,"
And scampers off with that.

She reaches up to be held
When sad or on a shelf,
And loves to see her Daddy's smile
At just being her eager self.

If in the midst of running around
She gets lonesome, missing Dad,
She stops, and seeks Him out - 'til found;
Then looks at Him, 'til glad.

Words nor thoughts can express what she sees
In His eyes and face;
She is refilled with His presence
And she lives in His grace.

She knows Her Lord is big and great,
He's powerful and smart;
Yet she snuggles up in His arms of love
And trusts her Daddy's heart.

The Lord also used my Pastor, Mike Lewis, as counselor. When I expressed that "I felt the Lord was making me walk through this," Pastor Mike asked, "Can you change the focus of this experience from feeling the Lord is forcing you, to feeling thankful that He did not allow you to stay the way you were?"

"You know," he added, "faulty layers can eventually destroy the purpose of an onion. Before this happened to you, God chose to change you, knowing that the onion beneath its bruised layers is still usable. To remove layers is progress. Growth. But to grow means to change, and change is uncomfortable. I believe that someday you will look back and be able to say, 'Thank You, Lord.'"

He further suggested that a small support group of local women my grandmotherly age might help nurture and sustain me. Within a week three precious ladies began meeting regularly with me. They held me while I cried, laid hands on my pain-paths, and prayed. They listened attentively when my hurts erupted. Never condemning, they just loved me and cared. These ladies, loving me as I was, hurting, crying and empty, expressed on the human level what God was doing in the spiritual realm.

It mattered to the Lord that I felt worthless inside, and that my trust in Him and others was out-of-focus. He communicated directly to me that He loves me and accepts me the way He made me. If the Lord approved of me, then I could begin to accept myself. I had value just because I existed – not because of achievements. I had nothing to commend myself to the Lord, but that was fine. All He ever wanted from me was the *me* He had created. His tender care during these valley months encouraged me to rest in Him and His plan for me.

Realizing I had worth as a person and finding acceptance, I began to relax. As I quit striving for approval, the Prince of Peace gave me the peace I so longed for. To allow Him to work *through* me, instead of my working *for* Him, relieved me of anxiety and the responsibility for the outcome. The more I rested in Him, the easier it was to obey.

As my new kind of trust grew and my hurts were attended to, health and peace began to emerge. Occasionally my appetite showed up, and my weight loss stopped. The pain – the horrible, unpredictable pain – began to subside for maybe an hour, then an afternoon, or morning. Eventually a whole day passed with no pain.

The tears that came as the result of my pain and weakness served as the root of my healing. My doctors never did pinpoint the cause of my excruciating misery. In trying to understand the "whys," I am as incredulous that there was nothing wrong physically, as I am that stress and emotions could cause that kind of pain. It is also hard to understand that pain can be used to heal wounded emotions.

I choose to believe God was doing just what He said – peeling off another layer to bring forth something new. And layer removal is serious surgery!

I acknowledge anew the truth that the Lord is in charge. His peace is calming like the azure sky above. He is the Prince of Peace, and He does answer prayer. He can use anything to remove bruised layers of hurt, the rotting layers of inferior feelings, and the misformed layers of trust, to move us from His permissive will to His perfect will. And now my grateful onion heart says without reservation, "Thank You, Lord."

SCRIPTURES and NOTES

72 Isaiah 9:6

For unto us a Child is born, unto us a Son is given; and the government will be upon His shoulder. And His name will be called Wonderful, Counselor, Mighty God, Everlasting Father, Prince of Peace.

73 Judges 6:23-24

Then the Lord said to him, Peace be with you; do not fear, you shall not die.

So Gideon built an altar there to the Lord, and called it The-Lord-is-Peace. To this day it is still in Ophrah of the Abiezrites.

74 1 Samuel 25:6

And thus you shall say to him who lives in prosperity: Peace be to you, peace to your house, and peace to all that you have!

75 Colossians 1:17

And He is before all things, and in Him all things consist.

76 Philippians 4:13

SHEEP IN STORM

God had said He was peeling off my wrong layers of trust (like onion layers). Weak and sick, I prayed, *"Would You give me a picture of You to carry me through this time?"*

The Lord wearing a long, hooded coat is slowly going up a hill covered with winter bushes and shrubs on a dark blue, icy, snowy night, slowly moving forward with His staff in hand.

I am a lone, scraggly, weak sheep blinded by the weather trying to follow Him by hearing His encouraging voice. He is with me and He is leading, but I must walk through this storm, following Him.

This time He cannot carry me by lifting me out of all this, but He is carrying me in a larger sense by loving me into greater trust and victory.

PUMPKIN
The Color of Goodness

Pumpkins come in all shades and sizes but mainly they are roundish, dressed in a dull, yellowish-orange color. Pumpkins add the finishing touch to harvest time in the fall. They remind us to offer thanks to the Lord for His bountiful blessings.

As a little red mixed with yellow makes a pumpkin color, a little love of God mixed with His light reveals Him as the God of abundance and goodness. This is certainly evident in His care of the natural world of plants, trees, stars, seas, and animals.

On the third day of creation, "El Roi," the-God-who-sees,[77] set up seedtime and harvest[78] as part of His overflowing goodness to man. We find security in His promise, "While the earth remains, seedtime and harvest, cold and heat, winter and summer, and day and night shall not cease."[79] Our soul's selfish desires, inadequacies, imbalances, and inner hurts decrease in the presence of His Goodness. God wants to supply all the needs of our bodies, souls, and spirits.[80] Though it blesses us, that is not the main reason He reaches out to us. Because "the Lord is good,"[81] He cannot deny Himself.

This story is about the Lord's goodness to Jeremy and me. As you may recall, Jeremy is the toy fox terrier who moved with me from Illinois to South Carolina 10 years before. The following "Thank You" was sent by Jeremy in April 1996 to the Dorchester Veterinary Clinic. Between his verses, I will fill in the details of what really was happening to occasion this thank you.

I have a secret deep within,
You'll never get it out of me;
Of how I escaped from a fenced-in yard
That was padlocked with a key.

As I came in from teaching a Bible Study at my church on a Tuesday morning in March, I called out to my toy fox terrier, "Jeremy, I'm home," No doggy response! For 11 years he had greeted me by running back and forth at break-neck speed, eager to see me, and hoping for a doggy treat. Fearful that he might be ill, I began to look for him in all his favorite places. Because we had a pet door allowing him access to the back yard, I went out there to search. I noted that the padlock was still intact on the gate latch of the chain-link fence. However, the latch seemed – possibly – slightly askew.

I was looking for my owner;
Who said she was going to church.
I got tired of waiting for her
And set out on my own to search.

Maybe he got out somehow so he is not too far away, I thought. I unlocked the gate and left it open, so he could easily get back in. I grabbed the car keys and headed out. I reminded the Lord as I drove along, *"He is a house dog and does not know about cars and streets and such. He is not wearing his collar and tags. If dogs have angels, would You send one to take care of Jeremy?"*

Because of the scent of her car
I could tell the way she went.
Beyond our neighborhood I ran
To find her, as if I had been sent.

On one of my frequent trips home to see if he had returned, I called out to a next-street neighbor, "Did you see a small terrier pass this way today?"

"Yes, I did," she said to my surprise, "about 10 this morning. He was really in a hurry."

As I enlarged my driving area, every wind-blown paper appeared to my glancing eyes to resemble my white canine friend with the black patches. His black stubby tail and pointed ears combined to give him a perky look. His ear positions changed with his feelings, such as, at half-mast he felt cornered. When I held him close and whispered to him, his ears flattened against his head as he sort of melted and leaned limp-like against me. Cutting his toenails remained an ordeal for he considered them off limits to me, but he liked to be brushed. His smooth coat needed it for he shed year around covering everything I owned with his short black and white hairs.

I named him Jeremy, meaning, "Appointed by the Lord." I believed he was a gift, and the perfect dog for me. His independent terrier personality pleased me, yet he demanded the same kind of loyalty he gave. He was all that I had hoped for in a pet. I was planning on our being together for a 100 "doggie" years or more. (That is at least 15 years.)

After traveling over yards and streets,
I came to a road with many cars.
With eagerness I sniffed and turned to the left,
Darting ahead, I felt a jar, and saw stars.

I searched all day until dark, then sat on my deck hoping to hear Jeremy's bark as a mother does her baby's cry. I felt betrayed. Wasn't he happy here? Why else would he leave? Finally it was 11 PM and time to close down the day – with no dog, and hope fading fast.

Lying in bed, I recalled a game we played. I would grab one of his feet and say, "This foot is mine." Immediately he would pull it back as if to say "No way will I trust you with that foot!" Then I would laugh and respond, "Since all of you is mine, I obviously own that foot, so you can trust me with it."

Those words suddenly echoed deep down inside where nobody but God sees. When problems with people, money, or health came, I shifted into a pulling-back mode. In effect I was saying to the Lord, *"No way will I trust You totally with that."* My faith was in the Lord, but trusting Him no matter what[82] was still hard.

Knowing I could do nothing more, I lay there probing the darkness with questions such as, "Wonder where Jeremy could be? Wonder if the Lord is doing anything about this? Does the Lord feel betrayed by my lack of trust as I feel betrayed by

Jeremy's leaving? Could the Lord have been seeking my trust even more intently than I have been seeking Jeremy?"

Tired of searching for answers, I finally leaned limp-like against the Lord, whispering,

> *Unless You can do something, Jeremy is gone for good, but I trust You with this, no matter what.*
>
> *I do not understand why, but You said "to give thanks in all things."*[83] *So, Lord, I thank You for Jeremy and for this situation. Jeremy's feet are Yours wherever they have taken him, . . . and so are mine.*

Relaxing, I soon drifted off to sleep.

I was knocked down and lay on the road
Before someone rescued me.
Thanks for caring enough to stop –
It was life or death, you see.

Wednesday morning at daylight, I awakened with the hope that maybe he had returned during the night, – but, alas, no dog in the house or yard. I dressed, grabbed a bite to eat, and resumed my searching.

Our neighbor took his dog to the same vet
And heard talk of a wounded "stray."
He hurried home to tell my master-ette –
I will never forget that day!

About 11 a.m. as I pulled into my drive, my neighbor, Jimmy, walked over to my car, and asked if I had found my dog yet. Then he handed me a card from the Dorchester Veterinary Clinic. He said, "I took my dog to have her stitches removed this morning. I overheard a phone call about a black and white stray who had been hit by a car. I thought you might want to check it out."

Hurriedly I thanked him. With heart pounding I called the clinic. My description sounded like the stray dog. I drove as fast as I dared and waited breathlessly to see the wounded pet. They explained that the stray had no broken bones, but his head had been traumatized.

When the hurt dog was brought to the room where I was . . . "Jeremy!" Emotions reduced me to tears. I fought to regain composure, managing a "Hi, Jeremy. Are you hurting?"

He started whining and part yelping. He leaned his whole 16 pounds against me as I encircled him with my arms.

"What happened to you? Did they give you a Milk Bone treat last night?"

More doggy response. I took stock of how he looked – swollen right side of head, enlarged cloudy eye, bruised skin.

Thanks for taking me to the vet
In my weak and helpless condition
I'm sorry I disrupted your day –
Disobedience was not my intention.

The vet said, "The lady who brought him in said he ran onto the road in front of a car."

"Is he going to be all right?" I asked.

"We are not sure about his eye, but otherwise he will be fine."

"When may I take him home?"

The vet explained, "The lady who brought him in said she would pay the bill, so we consider Jeremy hers so far as our care of him is concerned."

"But Doctor," I remonstrated, "he's my dog. I am responsible for his escaping, and his medical care. Her getting him to you was more than enough."

"I understand how you feel," he said, "and we will work it all out."

So glad my owner finally found me.
But how could she leave me at the vet's
When I'm hurting, bruised, and swollen,
And wearing a surgical collar for pets.

Saying good-bye to Jeremy, I told him I would be back later to take him home. I relinquished my terrier to the vet. On my way home, spontaneous praise flowed from my heart. I thanked the Lord aloud for sparing Jeremy's life, and returning him to me.

The doctors kept me alive,
They were so good and kind.
But the God my owner talks to
Had something more in mind.

About 3:30 I answered the phone to hear someone say, "Mrs. Bard, this is Kelli from your Bible Study. I am the one who took your dog to the vet. I was following the car who hit him yesterday."

I interrupted, "Do you know who hit him? Where did it happen?"

"Yes," she said. "I saw it all. Margaret was in front of me." (Margaret Wehman, coordinator for ladies meetings, was the one who had asked me to teach the Bible Study at our church, Cathedral of Praise.) "Jeremy ran into her lane of 50 mph traffic. She knew she could not stop soon enough, so she drove over him, purposefully missing him with her tires. However, something under her car must have hit his head. Jeremy was knocked down by the time I pulled to the edge of the road. Before I could get to him, an 18-wheeler-semi drove over him, likewise missing him with its tires. A man walking nearby ran out and pulled him off the road. The accident happened about a mile from the church. Since I knew the local vet, I took him there. Margaret knocked on doors near where he was hit, searching for his owner. By the way I'm signing the release papers now."

An hour later the receptionist at the clinic called to say Jeremy was doing fine, and that the total bill had been paid!

"By whom," I asked incredulously.

"A lady named Margaret Wehman. Do you know her?"

Margaret's unparalleled comment when I called to thank her was, "It was the least I could do after hitting your dog."

I heard my owner say "Thank You" to God
For protecting even the least,

And for Margaret, who paid my bill,
Who mirrors Your love for man and beast.

The Lord saw my hurt, saw my dog's hurt, saw to his care, and saw that I found him.

The Lord's goodness had abounded, showing me I can trust His ways. I saw Him at work in those who were kind enough to stop for a wounded, untagged animal, and who knew me. God worked through the local vet who with loving expertise treated the "stray." God planned for my neighbor to be at the vets to overhear the phone call. He arranged the financial blessing of having the bill and medications paid for. The Lord restored my dog and healed him. I am abundantly blessed.[84]

Totally trusting Him must be something God values, for it seems He is continually searching for evidence of it in my life. My searching goes on, too – not for my dog now – but to know better the Creator of my dog and me. I want to trust His purposeful ways in everything, no matter what. God's Goodness cannot be surpassed, "For the Lord is good, His mercy is everlasting, and His truth endures to all generations."[85]

I came home the next day
To recover and to think.
I've signed this note "Cor-'dog'-ily yours,"
And added my paw print of ink.
Cor–"dog"–ily yours, Jeremy
My eternal gratitude, Shirley

PS Jeremy wore a protective collar, looking as if he were a space dog for about 10 days, but never recovered sight in his right eye. Jeremy and I mailed revised variations of his poem to Kelli and Margaret.

SCRIPTURES and NOTES

77 Genesis 16:13

Then she (Hagar) called the name of the Lord who spoke to her, You-Are-the-God-Who-Sees; for she said, Have I also here seen Him who sees me?

78 Genesis 1:11

Then God said, Let the earth bring forth grass, the herb that yields seed, and the fruit tree that yields fruit according to its kind, who seed is in itself, on the earth; and it was so.

79 Genesis 8:22

80 Philippians 4:19

And my God shall supply all your need according to His riches in glory by Christ Jesus.

81 Psalm 100:5

For the Lord is good, His mercy is everlasting, and His truth endures to all generations.

82 Psalm 62:8

Trust in Him at all times, you people; pour out your heart before Him; God is a refuge for us.

83 I Thessalonians 5:18

In everything give thanks; for this is the will of God in Christ Jesus for you.

84 John 10:10

The thief does not come except to steal, and to kill, and to destroy. I have come that they may have life, and that they may have it more abundantly.

85 Psalm 100:5

HOLY GROUND

During morning worship we were singing "We Are Standing On Holy Ground." Suddenly I felt the part of the rock I was standing on split apart and take me heavenward. I leaned back on "Something Solid" as I reached dizzying heights. All awareness of the church service disappeared while I basked in the Lord's presence. Numerous angels in dazzling white hovered and fluttered around me. Their brilliance lit the chasm below me.

As I became aware again of the singing of those around me, the angels faded and I was instantly lowered to where I had started. I watched the rock edges close as if nothing had occurred. I was awed beyond words.

DEEP-SEA TEAL
The Color of Provision

Mixing blue and yellow produces a gamut of greens from the palest to the darkest. Plunging one color, teal, to its depth gives us a deep, deep turquoise – a deep-sea blue-green known as "Cousteau bleu" by the French.

Mixing (the blue of) truth with (the yellow of) light resounds inside us as greens of different intensities and depths. Some experiences barely rock our boat whereas others capsize our lives. Way beyond disturbing our health and inner rest, we are plunged to the depths of our souls struggling to survive failures, violence, incurable infirmities, or deaths.

Through the hourglass of testing, the sands of believing "God will provide" trickle s l o w l y. I was to be tested alone, a tailor-made, individual test, almost impossible in its demands.

"There's been an accident involving your husband downtown. Is there someone who can drive you to MUSC now?" asked the Charleston County Police Chaplain on the phone.

With trembling fingers I hurriedly dialed two friends, one to take me, and the other to pray and call the church office. Moving from my desk to the closet, I stood there staring at my clothes, realizing I had no facts – *What kind of accident? Where? How seriously hurt?* But I had to get dressed. *My husband had gone to the Veterans Hospital for a checkup . . . yet he is at the Medical University of South Carolina. . .*

Talking to myself, I said, *"Shirley, find something, – anything to put on. It doesn't matter what, just get dressed so you can leave."*

Finally grabbing something, I said to the Lord, *"This is what last Sunday morning was all about, isn't it?"* With fumbling hands I dressed, recalling my unusual experience during the worship service. We were standing and singing, "I Stand In Awe of You," when I began to get inexplicable chill bumps from head to foot.

> Suddenly I saw the Lord dressed in a pure white, ankle-length robe, standing in front of me on an iridescent green hillside with an October-blue sky behind Him.
>
> He raised his arms toward me and said, "I love you." Immediately I was surrounded by His presence of love and felt literally awash in it, almost as if I might drown.
>
> I thought more than said, *"This is what it will be like all the time when I come to be with You."*
>
> He replied, "You are already in My Presence of Love all the time – all you are ever going to get. Nothing changes about that when you come here."

Then the picture was gone. Becoming aware that others were still singing, I joined them.

Puzzled, yet awed by this experience, I was not able to tell Norval about it until Tuesday night. His comment? "Wonder what it means, and why it came at this time."

Now I knew!

This was the next day, on Wednesday morning, August 27, 1997, that the Chaplain called. "I will be waiting for you at the Emergency Room entrance," he said after writing down data about our two married daughters in the area. As I turned the key in the lock of my front door, I knew – I suddenly knew – that I would never see Norval alive again. I said out loud, *"Thank You, Lord, for preparing me with Your presence of love."*

At the hospital where family and friends were beginning to gather, we learned that Norval had walked to McDonalds after his early morning lab tests. He was returning to the Veterans Hospital for his doctor's appointment. Halfway across the four lanes of heavy morning traffic on the Crosstown, he stepped into the side of a five-axle-tractor-trailer truck that he did not see coming from the left. He never regained consciousness.

The Medical University Trauma Team continued to work with him at MUSC for almost two hours, but was unable to overcome the results of his extensive injuries. The Police Chaplain helped me reach my son in Illinois by phone, and stood by, as I heard myself conveying the unreal reality.

Back home, my inner running monologue provided a bridge between the unthinkable and the truth. So many decisions – a funeral home and burial? *(Why do I need to think about that?)* What will I wear? Must contact Social Security and insurances. *(Do I have to take time for this right now?)* Who will mow the lawn? . . . Be the family's packrat? *(Norval, of course, he will be back soon. But he can't. He is gone forever.)*

I hurt deep down inside, in fact I was in pain all over. I could not seem to focus on much. My wandering mind pictured us getting married 38½ years ago and starting our process of "two becoming one." That journey had included the blessings of a son and two daughters, their mates, and six grandchildren.

Abraham sacrificed the ram the Lord provided in place of Isaac, calling the place "Jehovah-Jireh" meaning The-Lord-Will-Provide.[86] When my husband and I read this together, we believed and trusted the Lord to be our Provider. Our marriage had known stormy places as seen in cloudy finances, showers of health problems, lightning bolts of learning to relate, and sometimes thundering changes. Through it all, we had found God faithful, and able to provide.

My inner video jumped to other times showing Norval as a bi-vocational pastor, working with some of God's choice sheep; we still enjoyed many of those precious friendships.

I recalled our last conversation, just this morning before he left about 6:45 a.m. He hugged me at the front door, kissed me good-bye, and said, "I will try to be back to get you to your eye exam by 10:45."

"If you can, that would be great," I had answered, "but if not, I can drive myself. Do not rush if you are running late.

Come on home and rest, and I will see you at lunchtime. Bye." I stood on the deck and waved to him as he drove away.

By 10:45 a.m. he was with the Lord.

Just that quickly my life was changed forever. Overcome with grief, I sat in my rocker – the one Norval and I had reupholstered in the spring – and cried. I was surrounded and held by friends and family. Sadness shrouded every memory like frost on a windowpane. That night I prayed,

> *Lord, how am I to handle this loss of Norval? I guess just like I would eat an elephant – one bite at a time. Does seem tonight I am not even able to handle one bite of sleeping. And I am so tired.*
>
> *Seems I relax all the way down and come to the dozing stage only to be jerked wide-awake by what has happened. Sleep eludes me instead of providing the temporary escape I need.*
>
> *Tears are supposed to provide release, but I cannot tell they are helping at all.*
>
> *I have always been aware that Norval could leave me by death, or by choice. Then what would I do? Once again I identified with Job who confessed, "The thing I greatly feared has come upon me."*[87] *The brutal reality of finality hovers, undulating unceasingly.*

At first, the Lord's provision for me occurred in the normal course of events as loving friends, kind neighbors, and strangers passed through my door. They took care of food and cleanup, the ringing phone, and ministered in every way possible. Norval was an extrovert, a people person. Now our family was being blessed by reaping the benefits of his nature. My daughters made the necessary phone calls to a funeral home, the Social Security office, and the cemetery to gain the information we needed for decisions. Pastor Mike Lewis strongly urged me to get sleeping help from my doctor.

Norval was buried on Saturday in a mausoleum (that he and I had selected the year before) inside a chapel. I began the dreaded reversal of "two becoming one." Norval and I had made all decisions and faced crises together. Now that death had torn us apart, I was left widowed, wounded, and weeping.

Missing the security I had known in Norval's love, I sought proof of his love in his gifts – one of which wanted to stay in my lap. Jeremy, my beloved terrier who lived a year after he was hit by a car, had died in mid-May. I cried for days, feeling the loss deeply. Before long Norval encouraged me to think about a replacement. Scanning newspaper ads daily he finally found another toy fox terrier. The last day of May he asked, "Would you like to go see a dog? I've made an appointment, but it's up to you." Of course I went, realizing his love for me was reaching beyond his desire for no more pets. After a few minutes with the new dog, we both knew five-month-old (already trained) Christy would go home with us. She sat in our laps, licked our faces, and filled our hearts.

It turned out that she loved Norval, as much as me, which pleased him immensely. Now that Norval was gone, she lay by his chair, or on his old sock with a knot in it given to her for a tug-of-war. When I sat down, she whined to be held. Her warmth and softness soothed my raw emotions each time I wrapped my arms around her. She would sit as still as a statue until my tears subsided. Then she laid her head on my shoulder as if to say, "I miss him too." Christy is a living legacy of my husband's love. As preparation for this time and evidence of His provision, the Lord had switched my sick, aging pet for a new, loving one.

The first three weeks after Norval's death, I was like a zombie – almost as if I were someone else – or watching everything from afar. Norval was the talker in our home. He went to sleep talking and woke up talking. The house seemed unbearably quiet now. The role of widow was new to me – untested, unreal, unwanted.

On Tuesday of the third week, I awakened with the word "RESOLVE" imprinted on my mind. Receiving this as from the Lord, I resolved to do at least one thing each day. I began that day by separating all the accumulation on my desk since his death, into piles of "thank yous" to do, insurances, needed forms, and cards received. That weekend my brother, Hilton Baker, drove from Kentucky to be with me. Since I had not been able to emotionally make myself answer the questions on insurance forms, his visit was a providential blessing. He sat right there beside me at the dining room table 'til the task was completed. Our being together consoled me, and helped me focus on coping, not just surviving.

I felt the Lord's "presence of love" expressed in myriads of written and phoned messages from friends far and near. Their ongoing compassion not only cushioned my bereavement, but helped me relinquish who I was, in the quest of finding out who I would be.

Besides a modest life insurance policy, Norval carried three accidental death policies, two of which he had added in 1997. He had felt strongly led to sign up for one of these only a month before his home going which happened six months past his 69th birthday. If he had reached 70, the amount of money received would have been cut in half.

At the time of Norval's death, the emergency room bill was quite high. Two years later, between insurance payments and the hospital's help, I owed them nothing. God remains My Provider, unsurpassed and unparalleled!

The evidence that the Lord was there all the time, paving the way ahead of my coming needs, continued to pile up, encouraging me to keep on trusting Him.

Yet dichotomies of thought persisted. Like most couples we had, in fun, discussed who would outlive the other. After he died, I remember thinking, "I won that one," followed by the sinking awareness that "to win was to lose."

We were disconnected by death, yet I still felt connected because the familiar thoughts and patterns we enjoyed as a couple clung like static electricity to my mind and actions. The nitty-gritties in our lives, the unsolved, sometimes aggravating, things that continually sanded the rough edges off each other during our marriage, were no longer relevant. Our time together was over. My balance wheel was gone.

Looking at a tall angel on display in my kitchen, one day I said aloud, *"I have to be content with a replica while Norval's with real angels. He's enjoying the glories of heaven, and I'm left with grief."* Though blessed with the support of family and friends, I had to walk through this valley-of-the-loss-of-a-mate alone.

In my dreams at night I wanted him to hold my hand or hug me, in vain. I came to understand that our love could no longer be a mutually, fulfilling expression for us because Norval was living in a different dimension. But, I had questions.

Following my custom of prayer journaling, I prayed one day at my computer,

> *Lord, I know human love is full of contradictions, manipulations and selfish desires, but when Your divine love infuses with ours, does that mean our love somehow lasts forever, too?*
>
> *Is Norval's love still with me? It hurts to remember our human love, but it hurts worse to try to negate it. Are the married years now null and void?*
>
> *Can You help me, Lord? I am listening . . .*

Wonder of wonders, these words came.

> You are right in thinking that My love, even when infused with yours, remains an eternal truth. The three-strand-cord of love made up of your's, Norval's and Mine is not quickly nor easily broken.[88] After all, I loved both of you, saved you, brought you to marriage, and graced your home with children and other blessings.
>
> My love imprint stands forever. That's the kind of love Norval is walking in now. Your memories of your shared love joined with Mine are valid, sustaining, and will endure.

> But your memory also contains your married love. Human love operating on a purely physical level remains temporal, mottled with imperfections, spots, and wrinkles. Married love enriched your lives, and gave expression to your varied emotions. This is the part that stops when death parts a couple.
>
> Remember, even these memories offer affirmation of you, your choices, and your life. Hold your memories dear, use them to advantage by letting them bless you and others.
>
> Norval has always been in My care, but now he is free from earthly restraints. I wiped away his tears over his sudden separation by death. He knows I will do what is best for you.
>
> As you release Norval more and more to Me, you will gain life, purpose, and wholeness. I have done and am doing My part toward healing you inside and out. Keep on leaning hard on Me for everything. I love you, and I am guiding you.

From this point on I rounded the corner in the grief maze from benumbing pain and tears to find hope beckoning. My injured love tentatively moved forward, hoping for healing. The surface of my life rippled with poignant rememberings, rising from the deep undercurrent of his death. My family and I responded with tears when we heard the songs on the radio or in church that Norval loved, and often performed as solos with his God-given, trained voice. "Great Is Thy Faithfulness" was one of his favorite hymns, but he could be heard singing along with any song. If he did not know or momentarily forgot the written words, he substituted his own and went right on.

Norval had said through the years, "I am ready to go, but I am in no hurry." As he aged he added, "I do not want to grow old and be infirmed, or become incapacitated." God knew his heart, and evidently granted him his desire in a quick, merciful way. The questions of "Why did it happen?" or "Was it fair?" have not gained a foothold in my thoughts, nor has the anger that many feel. I know the Lord acted out of love for both of us.

My sandy belief that God provides has not only survived the hourglass of testing but was made stronger in the process. Beyond the deep-sea teal of bereavement lay His ongoing purpose for me. I shall always stand in awe of the Lord whose provisions for me are as perfect as His timing when "we" became "I" once again.

SCRIPTURES and NOTES

86 Genesis 22:14

And Abraham called the name of the place, The-Lord-Will-Provide; as it is said to this day, In the Mount of the Lord it shall be provided.

87 Job 3:25

For the thing I greatly feared has come upon me, and what I dreaded has happened to me.

88 Ecclesiastes 4:12

Though one may be overpowered by another, two can withstand him, and a threefold cord is not quickly broken.

CHRIST ON THE HILLSIDE

During worship as we were singing, "I Stand In Awe of You," I began to get chill bumps from head to foot.

Suddenly I saw the Lord standing in front of me on a green hillside with the sky behind Him. He raised his arms toward me and said, "I love you." Immediately I was surrounded by His presence of love and felt literally awash in it, almost as if I might drown.

I thought-more-than-said, "This is what it will be like all the time when I come to be with You."

He replied, "You are already in My presence of love all the time, all you are ever going to get. Nothing changes about that when you come here," and He was gone.

PASTEL GREEN
The Color of Compassion

In the rainbow, this lighter shade of green appears closer to the yellow than the blue. Because truth (blue) at the time of a loss or death is a heavy load that can crowd out other things, a great deal of light (yellow) is needed. Enlightenment can be seen in a clearing of confusion, or a gracious gift, or a desire being met, or humor in the unexpected, or the "a-ha" moment of understanding. Because pastel colors are saturated with light, they boost our morale, and offer encouragement.

Pastel green is restful and healing, like the words of the Psalm that says, "The LORD is gracious and full of compassion, slow to anger and great in mercy. The LORD is good to all, and His tender mercies are over all His works."[89] His tender mercies comfort in the midst of grief as He graciously provides what is needed.

Back in the spring, Norval had surprised me by asking what kind of car I would prefer when we traded. Not having an opinion, I began to look at cars as we drove around. I saw a few vehicles in a heavenly shade of light green that were breathtakingly beautiful. There was no doubt about it, I loved that frosted color, and probably leaned toward envy every time I saw that green apple-of-my-eye-desire go by. Norval was incredulous that I was more interested in color than the make of the car, but he added, "If we can find a car the color you want, then that is the one we will get."

My affinity for pale green shows up from time to time. For my ninth grade graduation dress I remember choosing a pale verdant material overlaid with filmy green nylon. My first car back in my single days was metallic green and cream. My bridesmaids had worn full, mint-green "Gone-with-the-Wind" dresses. One of my favorite current outfits was pastel green. Since I like and use many colors, I cannot explain why I feel a glow within when I am in or near this restful, healing color.

Decisions about everything (including a car) were mine to make now that Norval was gone. Both of our cars (his nine-year-old Olds and my 13-year-old Pontiac) were deteriorating and no longer dependable.

My family got together in a few days after the funeral to discuss my financial situation to be sure I would be all right. In discussing a necessary car trade, they suggested three things: a certain price range, a car not more than two years old, and making the change as soon as possible. Getting an electric positioning seat was a priority also, but color ranked first on my list for I wanted that particular shade of green!

My research on newer automobiles consisted of craning my neck if I spotted the right shade of green car in traffic. After determining that Ford was the maker, I went by the dealership and learned that the "Light Evergreen Frost Metallic" color was phased out after 1995. Thinking aloud, I said, "If you had a used car in that dreamy color, I would trade right now," but they had none to show me.

Curious about the interior color used with my exterior favorite, I looked into a pastel green station wagon parked on the grocery lot one day. To my delight I saw a darker green with a blue-spruce tinge that perfectly complemented the outside.

I started driving Norval's Olds because of the still functioning air conditioning, but felt as if I were trespassing. We had driven each other's cars when necessary, but now his car reminded me daily of my loss. I began thinking more and more about trading cars.

Having neither the strength, nor the desire, to go from dealer to dealer searching for my choice, I prayed,

> *Lord, Creator of all colors, You know how I feel about that glossy green, but it is only a preference, not a requirement. I commit this car dilemma into Your hands. Lead me to the car You have for me.*

I awakened one Friday morning about a month after my husband's home going with the thought, *It is time to see about a car.* Since I had to pass two car dealerships on errands, I stopped and asked in each if they had a used Ford sedan in pale green. Negative. I was not surprised because I had not seen many in Charleston.

On my way home at noon, I decided on the spur of the moment to stop at the Stokes Mazda/VW dealership about a mile from my house where a casual friend from my church, Sandra Malone, was a salesperson. As I drove up, she was coming out the door. After conversational amenities I said, "I am interested in trading cars. I know what I want so it should not take a lot of time, depending on your answer, of course." During our brief conversation my hand was searching in my purse for a scrap of material I had purposefully put there. Hesitantly I pulled out the swatch of pale green cloth that matched the shade I was seeking, held it out to her, and hopefully asked, "Do you have a '95 Ford in this color?"

She looked at it, then back at me, and with a twinkle in her eye said, "I have one here with your name on it! Let's go see it." I caught my breath as we approached a gorgeous green '95 Taurus with only 46,000 miles. Before I got carried away, I reminded myself to ask, "Does it have an electric front seat?" Affirmative. In fact, it had all kinds of electronic equipment, loaded and fully equipped.

"Next question," I continued, "what is the price?" Sandra said, "Would you believe this car is on sale this weekend, reduced by $2500.00?" She quoted a price that was very close to the amount suggested by my family!

While she went to get the keys for a test drive, I literally walked around this lustrous green "Jericho" praying. (Joshua in the Bible had led his troops to walk around the city of Jericho once a day for six days, and on the seventh they marched around seven times, shouted, blew trumpets, and the walls fell down flat.)[90] With heart pounding I walked around the car praying,

Lord, is it possible this is the car You have for me?

> *Make Your will so clear I cannot miss it. Thank You for handling this whole car situation.*

Lingering doubts began to dissipate as details fell into place, such things as the trade-in on my old car paying the sales tax. I did not feel quite so alone making this decision knowing Norval and I had already agreed on it. I would not have thought it possible to feel joy in the midst of overwhelming grief and sadness, but I found myself smiling again – about the car. Grief was not spent, but this inner gladness provided a respite.

As I sat there trying to absorb what had just happened – *that God had led me on this day to the location of the car He had for me in the right price range* – the scripture that came to my mind was, "Every good gift and every perfect gift is from above."[91] I am grateful to the Lord for providing not only the gift of a dependable car, but for giving me the car of my dreams. I felt the Lord was reaffirming me by saying in effect, "You are still important to me above and beyond your loss, and I do care about details, even down to your color preferences."

Sandra asked if she could keep the swatch of green material since it was a first in her experience as a salesperson! During the time I was signing papers and closing the deal, she went to look in the Taurus to make sure it was ready. As the finale of God making His will so clear I could not miss it, Sandra soon burst into the office excitedly saying, "Here is proof that the Lord had this car sitting here, waiting for you. Look what I found under the driver's seat." She handed me a gold lapel stickpin saying "Jesus Saves" in the shape of a cross, topped with a tiny dove.

What a joy it has been to be surrounded by this gorgeous color every time I drive anywhere, and to know that the Lord provided it.

Over the next several months when asked how I was doing, I usually said, "The only thing I know for sure is that the Lord reigns." Reigning and providing in love, the Lord graciously was working all things together for the good of everyone involved.

A new year is normally a new beginning for everyone, but 1998 was more so for me. When I awakened January 1, I said, *"Happy New Year, Lord."* I know it was a totally inane thing to say to the eternal Lord who is not affected by time, but I felt His resounding response within, "Happy New Year, Shirley." His returned greeting warmed my heart, and gave me a lift.

King David and I agree that "The LORD is gracious and full of compassion, slow to anger and great in mercy. The LORD is good to all, and His tender mercies are over all His works."[92]

SCRIPTURES and NOTES

89 Psalm 145:8-9

90 Joshua 6

91 James 1:17

Every good gift and every perfect gift is from above, and comes down from the Father of lights, with whom there is no variation or shadow of turning.

92 Psalm 145:8-9

OLIVE GREEN
The Color Of Comfort

Olive green. A drab color, not the rich vibrant green color of health and healing. All shades of green depend on mixtures of yellow and blue, as health depends on light and truth. Olive is distinguished by the addition of gray, as if a shadow comes to stay. God who made the innumerable colors of the rainbow is a God of Light, not darkness, shadows, nor grayness. However, He uses such things to jump-start spiritual growth.

Shadows can be good. A tree's shadow gives us respite from the sun's hot rays. Jonah was grateful for the plant God caused to grow at warp speed to shade him.[93] God's shadow is an abiding place,[94] a respite for our spirits and souls being restored. Good shadows provide comfort.

Shadows may be bad. Shadows conceal evil people and their plans. We avoid dark, shadowy places – just in case. Diseases hide also, and multiply insidiously. Every tumor, benign or malignant, starts in a shadowy place, growing in secrecy 'til it is discovered. Malignancy translates into the dire darkness of "You have cancer."

I had been a widow about a year when I mentioned to my internist that there was a small, hard lump in my breast. I had been aware of it for a while, but figured it was benign. Because I had been eating right, drinking lots of water, and getting enough rest and exercise, I thought I was immune to cancer. I was to learn that preventative measures never come with guarantees.

On the first anniversary of my husband's home going, I prayed,

> *I rejoice to have endured the year, but am puzzled about my weakness, and the sudden drops of energy or life force inside. Are my physical symptoms a result of*

disease, emotions, stress, demons, aging, infection, or combinations of the above? Help me, Lord.

In His compassion and mercy, He responded with,

I AM with you in sickness and in health; I can use you in sickness and in health. As in My Word, faith makes you whole. Your faith is a gift from Me for when You need it. The amount or kind of faith is not the thrust, but faith in Me activates your gift inside.

I give the doctors ability and knowledge, and use them frequently to accomplish My will. But I AM not limited to them, or by them.

Testing time is always hard, especially in the basic area of trust. Trust is inherent in loving Me. Keep Your eyes on Me and Your heart in My Word, and I will bring it to pass.

I asked, *"Lord, what 'it' do You mean? Bring what to pass?"*

I AM perfecting that which concerns you. Abiding in Me is your peace and joy. What is going on inside you is all part of My plan. This is not punishment, but pruning.

Faith in Me, and working with the doctors are basic. Use your fight to overcome. Do not let it dissipate in guilt, blame, or what-ifs. I AM refocusing you to accomplish My goals in you – goals in writing, living, and serving.

My internist referred me to an oncologist who, after initial testing, decided to do a lumpectomy. On a Tuesday morning the minor surgery was performed. Fully awake as the procedure was done with local anesthesia, I (who has never even contemplated such a thing), humorously commented to my doctor and staff, "You all realize that this lumpectomy is going to curtail my topless dancing for a while!" They, knowing me and my lifestyle, laughed aloud as they proceeded.

Doctor had said the procedure would take about 10 minutes. After a while, I asked, "Aren't your 10 minutes about up?"

Doctor: "Yes, but I must clean up this mess."

"Doctor, have you made a mess?"

Doctor: "No, you have, but I am nearly finished now."

I went home and waited the l o n g 24 hours ('til 3 p.m. the next day) for the biopsy report, vacillating between resting and anxiety, begging God one minute, and believing Him the next.

Wednesday about 2 p.m., I was surprised to see my three closest friends and prayer mates arrive before I was to call about the results. These "Angel Ladies" are the same ones who started meeting with me in 1994. They have continued to support me in sickness and health. At the appointed time, I called my doctor. I was stunned to hear, "The lump is malignant." In a state of shock I heard myself repeating to my friends what I had just heard. We cried together and prayed trying to absorb this reality.

Throat problems seemed enough. Losing Norval seemed more than enough, and now this. Thoughts crowded in, such as, I would have to face this medical problem without Norval at my side. I wondered if my complexion would change from a healthy color to an olive green as my daddy's had with lung cancer.

Two days later, three of my friends, my two daughters, the oncologist and his wife (who is his nurse) and I crowded into an examining room to hear doctor's recommendations. He felt a modified mastectomy would be best. He preferred to do a lumpectomy on the other side at the same time. We all peppered him with questions, seeking facts, wanting assurances.

But, my primary concern was not about the cancer. After the Lord healed my throat, I felt responsible to exercise stewardship over my/His throat by protecting what He had fixed. Thus my anxiety centered on the reality of an intubation tube being placed in my throat during surgery. I expressed this fear, saying, "I would rather keep the lump than do anything to cause me to wear a trach for the rest of my life." The oncologist understood my fear, and felt talking with the anesthetist would help.

Talk about olive-drab days.

I expressed to the anesthetist my paralyzing, almost neurotic fear arising from past throat surgeries. In spite of my best efforts to control it or be rid of it, this fear had again assumed mountainous proportions. Dealing gently with my fears, he explained, "When the intubation tube cannot be used, a mask can be placed on top of the voice box. The mask inflates filling the trachea as the anesthesia goes into the lungs. The procedure, used for the last 10 years, does not even cause a sore throat." When he assured me he would use a mask, then the cancer reality left the simmering stage to join the throat dilemma already at boiling point. At home I cried a lot, letting tears express my profound shock and fears. It was hard to believe that cancer came as a part of the baggage in my life.

My oldest brother, Carvel Baker, called to see how I was coping with this cancer storm. When I told him where I was, he recommended I stop hiding the cancer surgery behind my throat anxieties. I needed to face my cancer and say to myself, *"I have cancer. Now what am I going to do about it."* To ignore it was to endanger my life.

He added as we talked that I needed to switch my hate of hospitals and being sick to being grateful they are there to help me overcome this. He asked, "Could I change my thinking from, *'I do not have a choice now about surgery'* to *'let us get it out, and done with, so I can get on with my life?'*" He offered many positive suggestions, such as, talk to your body, re-activating its resources. Recognize and operate in the power the mind holds over the body by trying different thought patterns, including funny things. Get other opinions. Take time to make right decisions. Remember you have brothers supporting you, wanting you well, and loving you.

Reading everything I could about how others had dealt

with cancer, I came across this quotation:

Speak to Him thou for He hears,
And spirit with Spirit can meet –
Closer is He than breathing,
And nearer than hands and feet.[95]

I knew that breathing was the last human function to shut down when dying, and that I had nearly died several times. This quotation raised questions inside that only the Lord could answer. I prayed:

Lord, is Your indwelling Holy Spirit closer than breathing in my thinking? In reality, yes; in practice, evidently not. Would You help me move past the control my throat still has on all I do?

Would You give me a picture of where we are, and how I am supposed to act?

Immediately I saw the icy-coated peaks of the Alps or Himalayan Mountains in bright sunlight. A girl and a deer leaped from peak to peak, moving safely to each slippery top. The animal stays one leap ahead as the girl's ponytail bounced behind her with each leap.

Not understanding, I asked, "Lord, what does this mean?"

There are two traveling – you, and My Holy Spirit as the deer. You are not alone. There is no end to the mountaintops for they are Our provisions for you.

Use your strength and energy to overcome. Ignore weather conditions and other difficulties along the way. Stopping means death.

Keep moving forward to your goals with purpose. My power makes you as sure-footed as the deer.[96] I AM your Rock, present in your mountains clear up to the tops.

Letting go and trusting the Lord completely was still a work in progress. In the last three years I had frequently camped out in Psalm 91, finding strength and help. Now I had questions such as, *How could I get cancer when I had claimed the scriptures that promised "no pestilence or plagues?"*

Lord, I need to talk with You about Psalm 91. I really believed and trusted when You wrote that "I should not fear pestilence that walked in darkness, that no evil would befall me, nor shall any plague come near my dwelling"[97] *I know You said I should not be afraid and that You would deliver me. But, cancer HAS COME and has been growing insidiously for five years.*

I trusted You when You said it would not come to me. Now I am confused, and my trust is tottering. You know I never want to use Your Word as a club or manipulation. Did I claim that particular scripture apart from Your will? If I have an incorrect, hidden motive, forgive me. Is there anything You can tell me now? I am listening . . .

The Lord's calm, majestic voice started speaking; (I started typing):

Remember that not every scripture in My Word is applicable to every situation for every person because of My Will and theirs. Just because you were unaware of the cancer within does not negate those verses, or My love.

You did well to trust in My care for it is there, even in the midst of this difficult time. I have allowed this to accomplish many things in many people. It is a necessary part of helping My people to be pure in heart.

Other things are disturbing me; what do I do with this scripture "Be it unto you according to your faith?"[98] *If "faith is the evidence of things not seen,"*[99] *should I keep asking You for confirmation? Do I keep on walking in faith until I get a red light?*

> Faith is not all that complicated. It is looking to Me to provide for you and others. By acknowledging I AM your source, you please Me.
>
> My Word is true and truth.[100] You can rely on it because My Spirit hastens to perform My Word.[101] My Word is magnified even above My Name.[102] When your spirit responds to Mine within you as you read in My Word about faith, or anything else for that matter, believe it, walk in it, claim it. If a red flag is needed, I will wave it as I did this time.
>
> To trust is not sin. To be afraid to trust is, for fear is not of Me.[103] Your trust was not the problem. My perfect will, timing, and other factors may not make the result of your trust what you had hoped,[104] but your trust is not wrong. You cannot see the whole picture as I can,[105] so trust in Me is necessary to develop trust in your requests.
>
> Hesitant trust is one of your mountaintops to be overcome with Me. In spite of the icy slopes of your questions and doubts, come, leap from mountaintop to mountaintop with Me.[106]

As I surrendered to His love and care, there were three things I knew for certain. The Lord reigns whether I live or die. He is trustworthy and able, for nothing is impossible with Him.[107] He is with me and in charge of all that happens to me.

I asked the Holy Spirit to minister to my subconscious and/or unconscious state during surgery, and to guide my surgeons. A modified mastectomy was performed about a month later. I went home the next day, having needed no pain medication for there was no pain. Since the slow-growing cancer was contained, I have not needed chemotherapy, radiation, or medication therapy.

My sense of humor clicked in again after the surgery when

I told my doctor, "This mastectomy is going to cancel my topless dancing career for good!"

To my "son-in-love" Al (who is a nurse) I said, "If I keep losing my body parts in hospitals here and there, the pallbearers won't have anything left to 'pallbear.' Besides, my health insurance premiums ought to decrease with fewer parts to insure."

Recovering, I had difficulty keeping a straight face when I heard the following comments in my living room: "God is no prospector (respecter) of persons," and "I've got a hyena (hiatal) hernia."

In November I wrote this "Thank You" to the Lord:

My heart overflows in gratitude to You, Lord. You are my Source, my Companion, my Shepherd. Without You, I can do nothing. Testing time is a walk of faith, a just-You-and-me-God deal.

Walking on cancer waters is scary indeed. Thank You for healing my body after surgery, and for healings in my spirit and soul. When I think about this whole cancer deal, I am overwhelmed with Your provisions.

Your precious saints have been Your human arms, legs, voices and hearts, visibly fulfilling Your role as provider.[108] *Thank You for my children and their mates, my grandchildren, my brothers and their families. My family is a blessing.*

Dr. Bernie Siegel wrote, "This most traumatic of events (the death of one's spouse) is often followed by cancer or other catastrophic illness in one or two years."[109] This was certainly true for me.

Facing cancer, even the fear of cancer, is a drab time. An olive green, drab time. It is possible to endure this time of shadows, for the Holy Spirit dwells within to enlighten and comfort. Jesus promised His followers that "The Comforter, the Holy Spirit, will teach you all things, and bring to your remembrance all things that I said to You."[110]

Because cancer affects our souls as well as our bodies, our trust in God's Word and His power brings the healing we need.

SCRIPTURES and NOTES

93 Jonah 4:6
And the Lord God prepared a plant and made it come up over Johah, that it might be shade for his head to deliver him from his misery. So Jonah was very grateful for the plant.

94 Psalm 91:1
He who dwells in the secret place of the Most High shall abide under the shadow of the Almighty.

95 Alfred, Lord Tennyson, THE HIGHER PANTHEISM, (Nicholson & Lee, editors, The Oxford Book of English Mystical Verse, 1917), XV, 644, p. 19 cm.

96 Habakkuk 3:19
The Lord God is my strength; He will make my feet like deer's feet, and He will make me walk on my high hills.

97 Psalm 91:10
No evil shall befall you, nor shall any plague come near your dwelling.

98 Matthew 9:29
Then he touched their eyes, saying, According to your faith let it be to you.

99 Hebrews 11:1
Now faith is the substance of things hoped for, the evidence of things not seen.

100 Psalm 119:160
The entirety of Your Word is truth, and every one of Your righteous judgments endures forever.

101 Jeremiah 1:12
Then the Lord said to me, You have seen well, for I am ready to perform My word.

102 Psalm 138:2
I will worship toward Your holy temple, and praise Your name, for Your lovingkindness and Your truth; for You have magnified Your word above all Your name.

103 2 Timothy 1:7
For God has not given us a spirit of fear, but of power and of love and of a sound mind.

104 Proverbs 16:9
A man's heart plans his way, but the Lord directs his steps.

105 Proverbs 20:24
A man's steps are of the Lord; how then can a man understand his own way?

106 Song of Solomon 8:14
Make haste, my beloved, and be like a gazelle or a young stag on the mountains of spices.

107 Luke 1:37
For with God nothing will be impossible.

108 Isaiah 54:05
For your Maker is your husband (provider), the Lord of hosts is His name; and your Redeemer is the Holy One of Israel; He is called the God of the whole earth.

109 Dr. Bernie Siegel, LOVE, MEDICINE & MIRACLES, (New York: Perennial Library, Harper & Row Publishers, 1986), p 74.

110 John 14:26
But the Helper, the Holy spirit, whom the Father will send in My name, He will teach you all things, and bring to your remembrance all things that I said to you.

LEAPING ON MOUNTAINS

Faced with cancer and surgery, I prayed,"Would You give me a picture of where we are, and how I am supposed to act?"

Immediately I saw the the icy-coated peaks in bright sunlight of the Alps or Himalaya Mts. A girl and a deer were leaping from peak to peak, moving safely to each slippery top. The animal stayed one leap ahead as the girl's ponytail bounced with each leap.

Not understanding, I asked, "Lord, what does this mean?"

There are two traveling – you, and My Holy Spirit as the deer. You are not alone. There is no end to the mountaintops for they are Our provisions for you. My power makes you as sure-footed as the deer. I AM your Rock, present in your mountains clear up to the tops. Use your strength and energy to overcome. Stopping means death. Ignore weather conditions and other difficulties along the way. Keep moving forward to your goals with purpose.

AMETHYST
The Color of Merciful Giving

An amethyst's color can range from a rich purple to a faint mauve. The word "amethyst" evolved from the Greek, meaning "not drunken," to symbolize sobriety. It was believed that this gem gave good things to its possessors, such as bringing victory, dispelling evil thoughts, and encouraging piety. This purple jewel also symbolized royalty.

What is believed to be true about the amethyst ***is*** true about our Lord. An amethyst is just a stone, but the Lord is the Rock of the ages, the eternal Rock of Royalty. He victoriously conquered Satan, sin, and death on the cross. Then the living God gave us His glory,[111] His victory,[112] His name,[113] His power,[114] and all things to enjoy.[115]

The God-head Trinity innately gives. God so loved that He gave His Son.[116] Jesus Christ gave His life.[117] The Holy Spirit is a Gift[118] who, in turn, gives all kinds of spiritual gifts.[119]

One area I knew very little about was spiritual gifts – what they were, or how they were used. In reading Romans,[120] I found seven gifts, namely, prophesying, serving, teaching, encouraging, giving, leading, and showing mercy. In I Corinthians[121] I saw how God uses these gifts.

More than curious, I wanted to know what spiritual gift He had placed within me. I confessed to the Lord that I could not figure out which of the seven gifts was mine, and asked Him to show me:

> I suddenly saw myself standing alone on the large protruding rock of a cliff. Without warning, everything to my right disappeared – no ground, no distant horizon – just a misty, bottomless, open chasm. I was not afraid, but I did not understand what I was seeing. Without my saying anything, the words of a hymn came to my mind: "There's a

> wideness in God's mercy like the wideness of the sea."[122] Then the picture was gone.

God's mercy? Here was something about God that I needed to pursue. Studying about it, I learned mercy is withholding the punishment deserved because of our sin nature inherited from Adam. "There is a wideness in God's mercy" because Jesus, the sinless Lamb of God, took the punishment for all people of all time when He died on the cross. Mercy, like all of the Lord's attributes, is an inherent part of His nature and shines forth continually.

Showing mercy is one of the seven spiritual gifts the Lord gives to minister to others. Mercy is shown by empathizing with anyone in need anywhere. Sympathy says I care. Compassion says I am sorry; is there anything I can do? Empathy says I identify with your suffering, as if I were in your skin with you. The merciful ones hold your hands, listen to your struggles, bring understanding to your mental distress, cheerfully walk with you, and rejoice with you over good things. They prefer to encourage from a quiet place, serving in the background with no fanfare.

The merciful take comfort in the words Jesus said, "Blessed are the merciful, for they shall obtain mercy."[123] The merciful willingly give of themselves to others, but they withdraw in the presence of insincere, unkind, dogmatic, or dictatorial persons. Because sharing the burdens of others can be a heavy drain on the merciful by loading them down, they are admonished to "show mercy with cheerfulness."[124]

This all sounded familiar because it defined how I felt inside. Yes, I could see that mercy was my spiritual gift, already active. My spiritual bent had opened the stage curtain allowing my mercy-gift to be already performing on the stage of life.

Showing mercy is not limited to the merciful-gifted. Many caring people walk in other's shoes (so to speak), and find ways to help. For example, in the spring of 1984, I had done some clothing alterations for a casual friend named Helen. She picked up on our financial stress, and offered us her cabin, pontoon boat, and canoe at Kentucky Lake for a vacation week's free getaway. I will never forget her merciful giving, nor the week there.

After the Lord revealed my mercy gift, I was ready to rush right out and minister in mercy to everyone in need. But, I was powerless to know how to go about it. I recalled that the disciples were told to wait in Jerusalem that they might "receive power when the Holy Spirit came upon them."[125] Maybe this was what I needed, but I did not know how.

I asked a friend, Joyce, at church to explain what it meant, and to pray with me. We both asked the Lord that I might receive the filling of His Spirit as evidenced by speaking in tongues, just like it says in Acts.[126] Absolutely nothing happened; my mouth gave no response, though I opened it, and waited.

One Wednesday morning in September, after my family had left for school and work, I went to my bedroom for my usual Bible study and prayer. As I was praying aloud, suddenly a rapidly spoken language flowed from my mouth. I was communicating with my spirit and mouth only, because I had no idea what I was saying. Evidently the Lord had honored my seeking to know Him by giving me another language besides English for prayer time. I had asked the Holy Spirit to fill me 14 years earlier, but the evidence of it came on God's schedule. I agreed with the Psalmist who wrote, "My times are in Your hand."[127] The something more God gave me this time was a prayer language, attesting to His Spirit's presence and work within.

Did all my troubles vanish? My problems cease? No. Daily decisions and difficulties continued, but I had peace within, a spiritual awakening. I knew the Lord loved me, and had heard my prayer. He wanted me to relate on a deeper level of knowing Him.

Allowing the bud of faith to flower into trust in one area does not ensure the development of other buds at all. Our spiritual and emotional growth patterns come individually in stages, spurts, and separate incidents.

The Lord God Almighty, the Giver of the ages, the greatest Giver of all had more to teach me about mercy and giving. He used what started out for me as a fun adventure. I ended up needing His help, as usual.

J. J. and I met in the spring of 1998 when both of us were searching. We soon became emotionally involved, in spite of different searches. As a widow of six months I was lonely, looking for diversion. He, a loner also, became a daily guest, and I looked forward to his visits. He must have felt the same way, for he returned day after day.

We looked nothing alike. He wore fur all the time, sporting a tall, feathery, furry-soft tail to die for. Yes, J. J. was a squirrel, and his search was for food. I obliged him by throwing out bread crumbs, nuts, or bits of apple. Standing on my back deck, I watched him from a distance of six feet as he munched away under the tall pine tree by my dining room window, buried food nearby, and did backward flips. When he chattered, I had no idea what he was saying. Nevertheless I talked to him about everything. He listened intently with perky, rounded ears in perpetual motion. He did not seem to find my presence offensive or threatening.

A creature of habit, J. J. always approached my house from across the street, and headed for my side yard. He left going through the chain-link fence into my neighbor's backyard. His coat blended brown and gray so perfectly I could not determine his color. His fascinating tail balanced him when he sat up, and blanketed him in the cold. Straddling a branch on hot days, his feet and tail hung straight down. He communicated "squirreleze" by twitching his tail in fluttering patterns. Viewing a sitting squirrel from behind, we discovered that the end of his tail makes a perfect circle. He was named by my granddaughter in kindergarten who remarked that his tail looked like a capital "J." Her older sister added the second "J."

One rainy day I saw the squirrel take a shower! The open end of the gutter on our back deck drained down onto the chain-length fence. He walked on top of the fence 'til he was under the stream of water. Taking his paws he washed his face, ears and chest. Then he retreated to the corner of the fence, turned around, and backed up to the water spilling down. After washing his backside and tail, he dripped his thoroughly wet body all along the fence 'til he jumped down to dry off.

Since the pine branch by the window was usually squirrel-free, I decided it was the perfect place for a bird feeder. I installed a green, hexagonal one with a pulley so I could add seeds from my backyard. The word traveled fast in the bird world, for I soon had cardinals, blue jays, flickers, sparrows, wrens, and doves enjoying the seeds either in the feeder or on the ground, dropped by careless beaks.

The first day the feeder was up, J. J. approached with all systems on alert. His whiskers and nose quivered. His tail announced. His beady eyes focused like a laser. Chattering continuously, he leaned out with hind feet gripping the tree trunk, grabbed the plastic roost, pulled the feeder toward himself, and ate his fill. He really liked bird seeds. By going directly to the feeder each day, he seemed to be under the impression that the seeds were for him.

This did not set too well with me. My "sweet-talking" became protesting and scolding – all to no avail. Only once did I win verbally. Discovering him at the feeder yet again, I told him in a disapproving tone, "Until you grow feathers and wings, the seeds are not for you!" He stopped eating, looked at me through what appeared to be tears, went up the tree, crossed my roof, and left. But the next day he was back. It was obvious to any casual observer that I was failing "Squirrel-ology 101."

Purposely I stopped throwing him crumbs and nuts, hoping to discourage his visits. Each time I refilled the feeder, I tried to hang it just out of his reach. When I blew it, the eating was easy. When I succeeded, he knew exactly what to do next. He ran across the branch, and down the rope holding the feeder. Then J. J. stretched past the feeder roof and ate.

I began to check the feeder frequently, in case he was "pigging out." If I knocked on the window at him, quick as lightning he would scamper to the trunk. If surprised, he might lose his balance and fall, landing on his feet like a cat. Undaunted he would climb right back up, and feast away.

J. J. developed immunity to my verbal barrage and window knocking. In frustration, I resorted to other strategies. Extending the adjustable pole of my ceiling duster as far as it would go, I banged on the fence or tree to deter him. His response was to go sit on a higher branch, hidden by the tree trunk until I went inside. My losing battle was no longer a secret between us, for sometimes I looked up to see my amused neighbor watching our chess moves.

Next I tried "Squirrel Away," a powder added to seeds that was safe for birds, but gives squirrels the temporary reaction of a head cold. Didn't faze J. J! Friends advised me to get a more expensive feeder designed to stop squirrels, but why should I have to buy a second feeder? Others said, "Just forget it. You can't win." But by this time, I could no more let it go, than J. J. could stop eating seeds. Our relating had taken a turn for the worse, for now we were competitors – competing for bird seeds!

But it was more than that for me. I was embarrassed to be bested by a squirrel. And insulted. I sympathized with the birds who came to an empty feeder. Helpless, running out of ideas on how to cope, I grew angrier and declared war. I was going to win, or else!

Except . . . what else could I do?

One day I found myself telling the Creator of birds and squirrels all about this problem:

> *The reason for the feeder was so I could see birds. I hated the unfairness to the birds. My anger was out of bounds. I felt helpless.*
>
> *I reminded Him that I had always enjoyed squirrels, and really cared about J. J. I was giving up on what to try next, and asked Him for help.*

In the quietness of that moment, I heard a voice deep down inside,

> *Is this the best use of your time and energy? Constant vigilance defeats the purpose of your enjoying this adventure. If you cannot handle the unfairness as you say, seek other options, but do not spend your energy in anger over this.*

What a difference those few words made – both by diffusing my anger, and giving me hope. Checking out other options, I chose an inexpensive, dome-shaped, 15" squirrel baffle in dull black plastic. Greasing the topside, I installed the free-moving barricade above the feeder roof. J. J. seemed as puzzled by the dome as he had been by the feeder at first. After stretching out toward the out-of-range feeder, he moved to his usual "Plan B" by going down the rope to the baffle. He gingerly put one foot on the slick black thing. It moved, and he jerked back. He tried again. Then in stretching toward the edge of the dome, he fell off! Three times he fell before he gave up, and left in defeat. The dome-shaped baffle was a good option. Meanwhile inside the house, I reacted with a yes-fisted gesture. After losing for two years, I was now winning!

Hope must spring eternal in J. J.'s heart, too, for he returned daily. I came home one day to find him on the trunk, chattering at one end, tail agitating at the other. My curiosity piqued, I looked toward the feeder. It was gone! Hurrying to the window, I saw the pulley, rope, baffle, feeder and seeds on the ground plus the broken connection. The upset birds were flitting from fence to branch. My nagging Blue Jay, who hollers "Jay, Jay" when out of seeds, joined J. J. in repetitiously expressing his dismay. Wanting to make things right for my creatures of habit, I got my ladder and reattached the pulley to the branch with a metal chain. I reconnected the baffle over the feeder, and replenished the bird seeds.

From J. J.'s point of view, he was hungry all along just like the birds. J. J. reclaimed my heart when, in spite of being denied seeds, he told me about the feeder. I have come full circle to loving him again. Anticipating his visits, I once again throw "squirrel goodies" on the ground. We no longer compete for seeds. Sometimes, purposely, I leave the feeder closer to the tree, so the ever-hopeful J. J. can feast on seeds. We have each found what we were searching for, making us both winners.

In spiritual realms, the battle was the Lord's. He reached my heart through my love of His created feathered and furry friends. I found myself seeing things from J. J.'s perspective, too – the mercy approach of "walking in his skin." God's lesson reached inside me, replacing anger, with the double-pronged thrust of giving and mercy.

My original rainbow continued to grow as this new shade of God's nature revealed His Merciful Giving. Jesus said, "Freely you have received, freely give."[128] It is as clear as an amethyst that giving is a "God thing" – a royal, victorious way of showing mercy.

SCRIPTURE and NOTES

111 John 17:22

And the glory which You (Father) gave Me I have given them, that they may be one just as We are one.

112 1 Corinthians 15:57

But thanks be to God, who gives us the victory through our Lord Jesus Christ.

113 Acts 11:25-26

Then Barnabas departed to Tarsus to seek Saul. And when he had found him, he brought him to Antioch. So it was that for a whole year they assembled with the church and taught a great many people. And the disciples were first called Christians in Antioch.

114 Luke 10:19

Behold, I give you the authority to trample on serpents and scorpions, and over all the power of the enemy, and nothing shall by any means hurt you.

115 1 Timothy 6:17

Command those who are rich in this present age not to be haughty, nor to trust in uncertain riches, but in the living God, who gives us richly all things to enjoy.

116 John 3:16

For God so loved the world that He gave His only begotten Son, that whoever believes in Him should not perish but have everlasting life.

117 John 10:18

No one takes it from Me, but I lay it down of Myself. I have power to lay it down, and I have power to take it again. This command I have received from My Father.

118 Luke 11:13

If you then, being evil, know how to give good gifts to your children, how much more will your heavenly Father give the Holy Spirit to those who ask Him.

119 1 Corinthians 12:1-6, 28-31

120 Romans 12:1-8

121 1 Corinthians 12:7-27

122 Frederick W. Faber, "There's a Wideness in God's Mercy," 1862

123 Matthew 5:7

124 Romans 12:8

He who exhorts, in exhortation; he who gives, with liberality; he who leads, with diligence; he who shows mercy, with cheerfulness.

125 Acts 1:8

But you shall receive power when the Holy Spirit has come upon you; and you shall be witnesses to Me in Jerusalem, and in all Judea and Samaria, and to the end of the earth.

126 Acts 2:4

And they were all filled with the Holy Spirit and began to speak with other tongues, as the Spirit gave them utterance.

127 Psalm 31:15

My times are in Your hand; deliver me from the hand of my enemies, and from those who persecute me.

128 Matthew 10:8

Heal the sick, cleanse the lepers, raise the dead, cast out demons. Freely you have received, freely give.

YALE BLUE
The Color Of Enabling

Yale blue falls between royal blue and navy. It designates a shade of blue chosen by Yale University in 1894. It has become a standard flag color used by nations around the world, including Israel. Called a dark sky-blue, it colors the stripes and Star of David on the Israeli flag and prayer shawl. The blue represents the truth of the Torah, the white stands for purity, and the Star of David symbolizes rebirth and new life for the Jewish people in the State of Israel.

This attention-getting shade of Yale blue so ably expresses the zeal and intensity the Jews have for the Lord God Almighty. God chose the city of Jerusalem[129] in the land of Israel[130] for His people to worship His great name. He has sustained their race throughout history, with and without miraculous intervention. No wonder the Jews call Him Jehovah-Shammah, meaning "God is present."[131] His presence is there, and He is there for them. The Lord remains their enabler.

The Lord is my enabler, too – as you shall see. In December 1999, Larry Lewis, one of our pastoral leaders, asked if I had thought about going to Israel in the spring with our church group. I said, "Not seriously," but promised to pray about it.

On the way home from errands one Saturday, the Lord said to me out of the blue, "You are going!"

I asked, *"Are You sure? You know I am not a good traveler, and I don't have the money."*

The Lord said nothing more.

Larry waited until I told him what the Lord had said before he confirmed it by saying he had heard the same from the Lord. Larry added my name to the list, and said, "Make your plans and trust the Lord to provide the funds."

I began to feel inferior to the paying members of this trip. Embarrassment and feelings of inadequacy surfaced every time I thought about others paying my way. At this point I was a stingy receiver. I told the Lord I figured the reason it was "more blessed to give"[132] was because it was so difficult to receive.

One day a friend said, "I cannot go this year, but I sure am excited about your going. I am thrilled to help pay your way." Her words opened my eyes to what the Lord was doing. I quit fretting about it . . . until Larry said we would need to pay for the entire trip by the end of January! He had received donations for me, but nowhere near enough to pay for the trip. He suggested I put the entire amount on my Visa card, and I nearly fainted. "What if the funds do not come in?" I asked, going on to say "I would never be able to pay off that bill. That is like going out on a tree limb, then chopping it off." Larry's response? "Either He is God, or He isn't. Are you going to trust Him to provide for you, or not?"

Accepting his challenge, I paid for my trip by Visa the next morning, praying,

> Lord, You are God and I am trusting You for this trip. I am going to Israel, seeking more of You and Your Presence. I do not have to go anywhere for this to happen, but I receive the truth that this trip is Your gift to me. I realize what I am seeking from You is not to be found in Israel or anywhere on this earth, but in the Person of Jesus, the beloved Son of God.
>
> Would You allow me the privilege of ministering to You there while You are ministering to me? As I walk where You walked in Israel, would You walk inside of me, over the hills and valleys of my soul, making straight the pathways for Your reign?
>
> As I am refreshed by the water there – the Sea of Galilee, Jordan River, and Dead Sea – would You pause within me and be refreshed by the living water flowing from Your Holy Spirit through my spirit?
>
> As I find respite in the villages, gardens and cities of Israel, would You make Yourself comfortable in the garden of my heart, feeding on what

> You have placed there and what You have cleansed?
>
> Lord, I want to know You and the power of Your resurrection, to be filled with Your Divine Presence while there, to glorify You. I also offer You myself, withholding nothing, hoping You will find a place to reign and rest inside of me there, . . . and here, when I return.

Larry encouraged me by letting me know as the money came in. Two weeks before we were to leave he gave me a check for the full amount, which I immediately deposited in my Visa account. Friends at church handed me cash to spend there. By the time I left, I had about $600.00 – exactly what I needed for taxes, tolls, fees, lunches, bottled water, and souvenirs.

The Lord provided for my needs as I prepared for the trip. A lady from our church said she would stay with Christy (my dog) each night. My daughter Shannon loaned me her large luggage with wheels.

The Lord's care continued while on the trip. He provided a walking partner for me. A young man by the name of Lyde Andrews offered me his arm and matched his steps to mine all over Israel. Lyde's physical support made it possible for an "out-of-breath-me" to get to each site. Though we arrived last each time, he deftly maneuvered me closer to hear our guide. I thank the Lord for Lyde.

You would think after the Lord provided so perfectly for my trip that my trust would be at an all-time high. It was. However, faith becomes trust in one area at a time. My spiritual and emotional growth patterns have come in stages, spurts, and separate incidents. The Lord, knowing my hidden, fearful ways, used a camel in Israel to stretch my trust a hump more.

"There are camels in the lobby," my roommate, Ginny, cried out as she burst into our hotel room. "I knew you would want to see them up close." By the time we got down there, the owners had moved the camels outside so tourists could ride them up and down the street. I was captivated, watching the camels move in and out among pedestrians and traffic. Ginny asked, "Would you like to ride a camel?"

She and I were touring Israel with about 40 from our church, the Cathedral of Praise. We had already traveled over the northern part of Israel for four days while staying in a hotel beside the Sea of Galilee. Now we were in Jerusalem for eight days touring the southern area.

Our Arab bus driver and Jewish tour guide were good friends who catered to us, a busload of Gentiles! Riding along, our guide asked us, "Do you know what the expression, 'In God we trust, but tie up your camel' means?" After some wild guesses on our part, he explained, "There are pick-pockets here as in any crowded place, so your jewelry and money must be hidden securely – in other words, 'tied up.' Visible jewelry, fanny-packs, and billfolds are open invitations to thieves, like untied camels." At each site as we prepared to leave the bus, he would remind us to secure our valuables by asking, "Have you tied up your camels?"

I was watching from my hotel window when a tame camel got loose. The owner of the two camels had accidentally dropped one of the leashes. The loose camel quickly moved a few feet away to munch on green grass at the curb. Then, realizing he was free, he lowered his head slightly and galloped up the street at full speed right there in Jerusalem. The owner's friend nearby mounted his white donkey, spurred it, and clip-clopped up the street to where the camel had paused. He reached out and grabbed the lead, then man, donkey, and camel sauntered back together. So I guess one's money would be gone like that camel if not tied or hidden.

Would I like to ride a camel? I remember trying to do the "Camel Walk" as a child. I would start out with my feet side by side, then put my right foot around behind the left one and on past it by two or three inches, and shift my weight. Next I would move my left foot behind my right, on past it two or three inches and shift my weight again. As I repeated the process, my knees resembled a camel's when walking. Giggling at the sight, I would soon lose my balance and fall over.

Would I like to ride a camel?

Thinking *nooooooo* was almost automatic. My first reaction has been to play it safe, not take chances where I might be out of control, laughed at, or in danger. Fear of embarrassing myself kept me from learning to ride a bicycle until I was almost a teenager.

I recalled standing immobile the first time I saw a roller coaster, aghast at its speed, height, and dips. I kept returning to watch the speeding monster, secretly wanting to ride, but afraid to try it. Curiosity, or maybe desire, finally won out. I went from being totally terrified when it clattered up the first steep incline to enjoying the daring adventure by the time it was over.

I move like a sloth toward new concepts and actions. I have found support and comfort in the old adage, "Standing there like a calf at a new gate." In spite of the bovine implication, I knew I was not the only one who has balked. Others had also been guilty of *not* being "the first by whom the new was tried." A delayed reaction to trying something new may not be all bad, but it leaves me divided between dread and desire.

Now here was Ginny asking me about a camel ride.

I rationalized with lightning speed that *riding a camel was probably not a good thing for a grandmother to do... anything could happen . . .I would look silly . . .what did I know about camels anyway?* They are brownish and have one or two humps. *This camel has one, like all the others in Israel.* Some are good-natured and patient, but they can also be bad-tempered, spitting, and kicking. *Wonder what this one's like?* They can go about a week without water. *When did this camel last have a drink?*

Would I like to ride a camel?

"No, I don't think so," I finally answered.

Back in our room, I told Ginny that I would be sorry to my dying day that I had said "no" to the camel ride.

She replied, "As much as you love animals, I thought you would want to ride one, or at least touch it."

"I really did want to ride a camel, and do not know why I

said 'no,' other than I usually reject new possibilities. My family says suggesting new things to me ahead of time seems to be as necessary as lighting a pilot light." Adding as I turned down my bedcovers, "I do not want to be this way, I just am."

In the dark, my windstorm of thoughts kept the sandman at bay. I pictured the camels ready for riders, waiting . . . Rehearsing my disappointment in myself, I slowly unfolded the why of my knee-jerk "no's," and found *fear*, hidden . . . but looming as big as a camel.

Deep-down inside, I seemed to hear a looser translation of the Lord's words[133] that went something like this, "It is easier for a camel to go through the eye of a needle than for you to change your fearful reactions."

Silently I agreed. Fear, like a camel, had poked its head into the tent of my life, entered and taken over, leaving little room for anything different. Tired of fear's control, I prayed, *"Lord, I give up. I can't change my fearful ways. Would You take them, and turn my desert of fear into an oasis of trust?"*

I told Ginny the next morning as we dressed, "If I get another chance to ride a camel, anywhere, before we leave Israel, I am going to take it."

After breakfast as we headed toward our bus, I tensed up when I saw that the camels were back. I walked rather slowly over to where they stood, chewing their cud. Watching me watching them, the owner asked, "Would you like to ride a camel?"

Before I could rationalize my desire away, I blurted out "YES!" With heart pounding, I breathlessly confessed to him that I had always wanted to ride one. *(Secretly, I have wondered what it must have been like for the wise men.)*

After the owner made the camel lie down, I walked closer to this huge beast who was almost as tall as I. Puzzled, (seeing no a chair or ladder nearby), I asked the owner, "How does one get on?"

He took my hand and led me around the camel to its left side for mounting. Then he explained, "Put your left arm around my neck and I will take your right leg and swing it up over the camel." I did, and he did, and suddenly I was sitting in the saddle on top of a huge hump.

"Hold on tight," he said, "as the camel stands." I grabbed the 10-inch vertical pole in front of me that was attached to the saddle, and held on for all I was worth. The camel raised his back knees first to stand up on his hind legs, and I was sure I would topple off – right over head, hump, and all! Then as the camel unfolded his knees to stand with his front legs, I felt as if I were falling off backwards. Finally he was standing on his padded feet at full height. I was sitting about eight feet up in the air, aware that his head was still higher.

I took a deep breath, trying to slow down my adrenaline from the mounting. Then led by his owner, the camel started to walk. I discovered I was being rocked, similar to being in a rocking chair. The two legs on one side of a camel move forward at the same time, then the two on the other side, producing a gentle, rocking motion with a gait. Horses move opposite legs forward causing a bouncing motion, but camels rock one back and forth. What looked like an awkward gait was a relaxing ride. Calmer now, I enjoyed the ride. In fact, I loved it.

After the ride, I dismounted the same way I got on, only in reverse. Now I understood a little better how the wise men were able to ride camels for months in their search. In spite of their not knowing the way, they followed the Lord's star that eventually led them to the Christ Child. In spite of my not knowing the way out of fearfulness, I trusted the Lord who did, . . . and He used a camel to get me there! Knowing my desire to ride, He took my camel-sized fear, put it through my needle's eye of trust, . . . and gave me the freedom of an untied camel.

Back home I was reading Joshua three and realized the scriptures mirrored perfectly the way He had led me concerning Israel. My indecision about going was paralleled by the Israelites standing at the Jordan River before entering the Promised Land. Joshua and they needed to hear from God.[134]

Getting a word from the Lord was imperative to my thinking seriously about the trip. I recalled after our prayers for guidance God saying "You are going," and Larry's confirmation.

The priests were told to stand still and let God take care of the crossing.[135] I had to stand still and wait for the Lord to provide for my tour costs and cash. As the priests had to step into the Jordan River before the waters were stayed, so I had to put the trip on Visa by faith due to deadlines.

The Israelites crossed on dry land.[136] Two weeks before the trip, the Lord provided a paid-for trip as my dry land for crossing. He took care of every detail for me (dog sitter, walking partner, shopping in Jerusalem, and safety) the same way He provided the 12 stones in the dry riverbed for the altar the Israelites were to build afterwards.

Joshua said, "By this you shall know the Living God is among you."[137] By God's hand I was enabled to go, and sustained throughout the whole trip.

My Promised-Land trip was filled with "milk and honey"[138] from its onset. It continues to both challenge and satisfy my heart daily. Going to Israel changed me by giving me a more tender love for my Lord, and expanding my trust. My Bible knowledge was enriched, and my passion for Israel soared.

This Yale-blue experience taught me how to trust the Lord in the good times – for good things. Jehovah-Shammah (the Lord's Presence) was real to me in Israel, and is real to me now. The Lord is able, and He remains my enabler.

SCRIPTURES and NOTES

129 1 Kings 11:36

And to his son I will give one tribe, that My servant David may always have a lamp before Me in Jerusalem, the city which I have chosen for Myself, to put My name there.

130 Ezekiel 20:5

Say to them, Thus says the Lord God: On the day when I chose Israel and raised My hand in an oath to the descendants of the house of Jacob, and made Myself known to them in the land of Egypt, I raised My hand in an oath to them, saying, I am the Lord your God.

131 Ezekiel 48:35

All the way around shall be eighteen thousand cubits; and the name of the city from that day shall be: THE LORD IS THERE.

132 Acts 20:35

I have shown you in every way, by laboring like this, that you must support the weak. And remember the words of the Lord Jesus, that He said, It is more blessed to give than to receive.

133 Matthew 19:24

And again I say to you, it is easier for a camel to go through the eye of a needle than for a rich man to enter the kingdom of God.

134 Joshua 3:9

So Joshua said to the children of Israel, Come here, and hear the words of the Lord your God.

135 Joshua 3:8

You shall command the priests who bear the ark of the covenant, saying, When you have come to the edge of the water of the Jordan, you shall stand in the Jordan.

136 Joshua 3:17

Then the priests who bore the ark of the covenant of the Lord stood firm on dry ground in the midst of the Jordan; and all Israel crossed over on dry ground, until all the people had crossed completely over the Jordan.

137 Joshua 3:10

And Joshua said, By this you shall know that the living God is among you, and that He will without fail drive out from before you the Canaanites and the Hittites and the Hivites and the Perizzites and the Girgashites and the Amorites and the Jebusites.

138 Ezekiel 20:6

On that day I raised My hand in an oath to them, to bring them out of the land of Egypt into a land that I had searched out for them, flowing with milk and honey, the glory of all lands.

OPAL
The Color of Living Stones

Gem stones, valued for their beauty, stand apart from the non-descript stones used as basic components of buildings, streets, walls, bridges, and memorials. Among opaque gemstones are opals, shimmering with inner rainbow colors. The way opals respond to light depends on their inward composition and moisture.

In much the same way the true colors of our character and temperament are revealed in the light of challenge and adversity. We deal with the un-gem-like daily grind of hard choices and stony circumstances. Opportunities to shine by being heroic or famous or wealthy are as rare as fiery opals for most of us, but opalescence (iridescence) is attainable.

With its abundance and endurance, stone has been the obvious building material used throughout history. Archaeological digs bear this out for we see each civilization has built on top of the former, trusting the rock and stone underneath to make sure foundations.

Geologically speaking, the words *rock* and *stone* are not synonymous because stones are broken-off pieces of rock. Our Creator used rock to form the core of earth, making it solid and strong. Then He added layers of graduating hardness of rock from the inside out. On the earth's surface, rock is broken up by weather, erosion, earthquakes, volcanoes, and man. This brokenness produces stones everywhere in all sizes, colors, strengths, and durability.

In the original Hebrew and Greek scriptures stone is not used interchangeably with rock, nor is it a substitute for rock. King David declared, "The Lord lives! Blessed be my Rock!"[139] Jesus Himself said the foundation of His church was built on the solid rock (petra) of Peter's confession, "You are the Christ, the Son of the Living God."[140] In the rock-likeness of God security dwells.[141]

In contrast, mankind is stone-like, broken, and separated. A name like Peter meaning a stone, or a piece of rock in both Greek (Petros) and in Aramaic (Cephas) bears this out.

One in five scriptures mentions stones or rock, sometimes even listing their names. The lands of the Middle East are likewise filled with rock and stones. Walking through the gates of Jerusalem I was encompassed above, all around, and below with stone. I liked the comfortable feeling of being surrounded by stone. I better understood the Israelites' feeling of safety within their stonewalls and houses. Even Jesus' disciples expressed a sense of security in the stone buildings of the temple,[142] but Jesus knew stones only simulate security.

The satisfying feeling of being close to stone must have settled down deep inside me. After I had been home a few days, I was unaccountably pulled toward a gas log, brown, stone fireplace at a yard sale. The stones felt rough and cold to my touch. Bargaining for it (as I had learned to do on my trip to Israel), I became the owner of a real fireplace for $20.00, whose brown stones begged to be painted.

That afternoon it dawned on me (not a yardsaler) why I could not resist the fireplace. I was missing the all-encompassing stones of Jerusalem. Within a few days, I painted those brown stones with the palest blues, grays, yellows or pinks imaginable with hints of deeper shades in the cavities. I tried to duplicate the delicate coloring of the stones by looking at the small stones I had brought from Israel. A light beige-pinkish color for the mortar tied the pastel-colored stones in with my decor.

Setting the fireplace against the obvious wall in my living room, I was suddenly faced with a problem. It totally covered the only heating/air- conditioning vent in the room. Neither family nor friends had any ideas how to solve this dilemma.

When I finally remembered to pray about it, the Lord gave me the perfect solution. He reminded me deep inside "that most fireplaces have hearths." Of course – a hearth would raise the fireplace off the vent. I built a rectangular hearth (12 inches high by 24 inches wide by six feet long) with supporting boards at the ends. The left support was moved in about 18 inches allowing unseen room for the vent. I painted the hearth to look like pale blue marble with faded straw-colored streaks, and set the fireplace on it. Thoroughly satisfied with the results, I was to learn that completing the fireplace was not the end of the story.

The Lord used my new fondness for stone as a connecting link to stretch my trust in Him further. In Jeremiah I read, "I will build you up again, and you will be rebuilt."[143] This verse even found expression in a dream.

> One night it seems I was in a large living room, devoid of furniture. I was lying on the floor holding the green steering wheel from my car. Nearby stood one of my car windows, and other auto parts. My deeper understanding upon awakening was that God was putting me together, piece by piece, the same way my car was put together, piece by piece. It was a graphic picture of how He was re-building me.

I seemed to be drawn to and riveted to Bible verses about stones and rock. In the New Testament, I found these words, "You, like living stones, are being built into a spiritual house."[144] This verse and the one in Jeremiah grabbed my attention, but not my understanding. I asked the Holy Spirit to show me what He was doing, and heard this response deep down inside:

> Your building is made of the experiences of your life pictured as stones. What has happened to you, plus your reactions has produced rough stones of many sizes. Your human understandings through the years have been limited at best, and misinterpreted, or wrong at the worst.
>
> You have tried diligently to alter, switch, and cut your own stones to repair troubled areas. Your additions and will-power decisions have left chisel

marks, but are of no lasting value. As you gain insights into your past, I will be reshaping your stones. Remember physical healing is a part of wholeness, but does not define it.

The mortar of your understandings as you have walked through life has set up like concrete between your unevenly stacked stones. Your experiences have been locked into set thought-patterns that have molded your building incorrectly.

I am chipping off and digging out the old, dried-up, cracked mortar that is misaligning your building. Then I will pour over you new mortar, the mortar of love. It is the right ingredient for wholeness because it is pliable, moldable, adjustable, and has permanent bonding.

My perfect mortar will hold in place the stones I am reshaping as I rebuild you. Your experiences (stones) must be surrounded and set in My mortar of love, so you will reap the true benefits.

The pain you feel is the conflict of warfare going on inside. Your distorted views and warped understandings will dissipate as My truth permeates your mind, will, and emotions. Your victories, seen as stones of differing sizes, will be rock-solid because you are building your house on the Rock of Jesus and His will for you.

Surround yourself with verses about My love for you, not yours for Me because at this point they would become works rather than trust. Keep them before you, meditate on them, believe them, and receive my mortar love. I AM your Carpenter with perfect knowledge of how to rebuild you. My "love has been poured out in your heart by the Holy Spirit."[145] Receive this gift as part of My rebuilding your house for My Spirit to dwell.

In learning more about trust, I was given greater understanding of His love. Love is not always gushy and sweet. Sometimes it is tough, and its down side is hurt. God the Father knew hurt.[146] Jesus experienced hurt on every level.[147] The Holy Spirit hurts and grieves.[148] To love is to be vulnerable to hurt, but the alternative is unthinkable. We need love to survive, grow properly, and overcome – both the love of God and the love of significant people around us. Love is given and giving, flowing from God to us, on to others, and back to God.

The love of God makes all the difference in the world to me. However, the Holy Spirit warned me not to let any one facet of our Lord become a fetish. Though God is love, love is not the totality of God's nature. Seeking only His love may cause us to miss *Him*, the Owner of this glorious love offered to us.

Rainbows come when light shines on mists and raindrops. Healing has come when His light shines through my tears, continually washing away hurts, heaviness, and stress. I want the Lord to keep on emptying my emotions of all past misunderstandings, misinformation, and mistaken identity. He can rebuild the stones of my experiences into any shape He desires.

Trusting who He is and what He promised is my part. He does the rest. When the Lord enlightens the spirit and encourages the soul, it is not long until the Living Water sparkles from within, making one opalescent.

SCRIPTURES and NOTES

139 Psalm 18:46

The Lord lives! Blessed be my Rock! Let the God of my salvation be exalted.

140 Matthew 16:16-18

141 Psalm 18:2

The Lord is my rock and my fortress and my deliverer; my God, my strength, in whom I will trust; my shield and the horn of my salvation, my stronghold.

142 Matthew 24:1

Then Jesus went out and departed from the temple, and His disciples came up to show Him the buildings of the temple.

143 Jeremiah 31:04

144 1 Peter 2:5

You also, as living stones, are being built up a spiritual house, a holy priesthood, to offer up spiritual sacrifices acceptable to God through Jesus Christ.

145 Romans 5:5

Now hope does not disappoint, because the love of God has been poured out in our hearts by the Holy Spirit who was given to us.

146 Genesis 6:6

And the Lord was sorry that He had made man on the earth, and He was grieved in His heart.

147 Luke 9:22

Saying, The Son of Man must suffer many things, and be rejected by the elders and chief priests and scribes, and be killed, and be raised the third day.

148 Ephesians 4:30

And do not grieve the Holy Spirit of God, by whom you were sealed for the day of redemption.

MALACHITE
The Color Of Nurture

Malachite is green, a mineral ore of copper used for jewelry, carvings, and pigment. Its name comes from the Greek word "mallow" which is a green herb. Malachite's diverse light and dark green bands may be opaque or translucent, making each polished stone unique.

In Israel where our tour bus stopped on the old Jericho road, I bought a malachite necklace from a Bedouin peddler. The individually crafted necklace has 12 malachite gems, plus seven silver-filigreed pendants, each tipped with malachite. Each of the 19 stones is unique and highly polished.

Green symbolizes growth and health. As green is the result of mixing blue and yellow, healing follows the mix of truth and light. But, growth may be a difficult and painful process, marching to the tune of change.

I am a spirit, I have a soul, and I live in a body.[149] Any change in one area disturbs the others because all three are intertwined in a delicate balance. Since nothing happens by chance, experiences come to us with the distinctive purpose of carving out, sculpting, or polishing away the dross and impurities of being human.

One of Malachite's dark green bands showed up in my life on my return from Israel. Someone has said, "After blessing comes testing." If the trip to Israel was a blessing, then bodily pain for months afterwards was the testing. I came home from Israel too excited and elated to slow down. Instead of taking time to let my body readjust by resting more, I went right into a full schedule of activities. I pushed to reupholster my couch, redo the fireplace, put together my picture album of Israel, and tell others about my trip – full steam ahead into exhaustion!

I had been home from Israel for only a few weeks when a

younger, close friend with a family from my church was killed in a car accident. I knew he was with the Lord, but I was left in mourning with no reserves for grief.

A month later my youngest brother, Joe Baker, died unexpectedly of a heart attack. He was the first of us four siblings to go. The stressful funeral trip to Kentucky was filled with air flight glitches, luggage delays, lack of rest, body misalignment, and grief. All this stewed inside without respite until I got home where I collapsed in physical bankruptcy.

I was still bruised from the 1994 death of my mother and wounded from the 1997 death of my husband. With family deaths, the emotional baggage from unresolved conflicts or unfinished business has to be dealt with as well as the loss.

As mentioned earlier my body responded to the grief and trauma of my mother's and husband's deaths by encircling my lower chest area with spasms of pain and fluctuating blood pressure. These symptoms abated over time. After the deaths of both my friend and brother, the pain returned with a vengeance, compounded by weakness, loss of energy and appetite, surges of high blood pressure, heart discomfort, and empty bowels.

All summer I had to force myself to eat even a tablespoon of food at a time. I dropped over 25 pounds.

My doctor ran all kinds of tests on my mid-section and tried different kinds of medicines. When testing revealed no specific problems, my doctor concluded that this was my body's way of dealing with stress, loss, and trauma. My physical symptoms were an indication of inner distress.

Evidently my body became the battleground where my spirit (the place where God dwells within) and my soul (the mind, will, and emotions) fought. Day and night I prayed for relief and healing. At one point I remember asking the Lord,

> *Is this pain and weakness a part of Your teaching me to trust You? Since I do not know what all is going on inside, I cannot evaluate the situation, but You, Lord, are living within me. You are in control of what happens. I need Your help, Lord. Is there anything You can*

tell me now?"

After this prayer, the Lord answered immediately and to the point:

Something must be lost before I can work. In the Old Testament, Saul's dad lost his donkeys.[150] Saul was sent to find them, but found God instead and His plans already in motion for him to be king.[151]

You have lost what? . . . parents, husband, brother, friend, control over your body, activities, time?

Remember He who loses his life for My sake shall find it.[152]

Forget those things that are behind and reach forward to those things ahead.[153]

In order to keep on working within You, I ask you, "What have you found?"

I felt a little like Job in the Old Testament when God questioned him toward the end of his time of testing, except my questioning was not as difficult. I expressed to the Lord that:

I had found His presence real. His provisions for me were unlimited. His love found expression through those around me. The scriptures were an unending source of pleasure and spiritual food.

Since the Lord knew my thoughts already, I decided to talk with Him about my fear of dying. I was not afraid of death, for I knew that I would be with Him. We would just be switching homes. Instead of His living here within me, I would be going to live with Him forever. So, I told Him,

When confronting deaths of loved ones, it seems I retreat inside. I admit that the loss of my brother has taken away some of my security. Such questions as Will I be next? Lie buried?– too horrible to contemplate.

Reality says death knocks more frequently as we grow older, but I am not dealing with reality. When I think

> *That could have been me I recoil in fear, clutching my mortality as if I could change things.*
>
> *I confess my pulling back, retreating, trying to protect myself. I let go of the right to live I have been holding onto. I throw myself on Your mercy, asking and receiving your forgiveness. My fight cannot be against You, but with You, against evil.*

The Lord also enlightened my understanding by speaking truth through my daughter. She pointed out that it was not my *death* I feared, but my *ceasing to live* that I could not accept. Like a laser, the Lord had penetrated my fear and pinpointed my problem through her. I knew I had not completed what I felt the Lord had called me to do. Therefore, dying was not on my agenda at this time (as if it were up to me!) My inability to handle my own dying caused my insides to shrink and shudder with emotional impact, bringing pain and weakness. My helplessness to change reality affected me physically. Thus, I was bringing into being the very thing I was trying to avoid. Once again I concurred with Job who centuries before had written, "The thing I greatly feared has come upon me, and what I dreaded has happened to me."[154]

God knew I needed His nurturing, so El Shaddai,[155] the "All Sufficient One, (literally the "Strong One, Breasted"), ministered to me by responding,

> Healing for you is going to take time, just as Saul did not find the donkeys immediately for a reason. In fact, he did not find them at all, but they were found!
>
> Physical healing is a part of wholeness, but does not determine it. I AM working within so you will be able to let go of tenseness, anxiety, perfectionism, fears of confronting, lack of energy, voice power, and death.
>
> No wonder your insides hurt. These areas have not come from Me. They do not allow room for My

> Spirit to work. The pain you feel is the conflict, warfare going on inside. Do not fear, or waste energy on useless resistance. Relax, knowing that I AM with you. I AM healing you, and stretching you as you grow. Your body will be helped with mild exercise. Make that a daily practice.

More positive input came from a TV preacher who said, "The facts are . . . , but the truth is . . . " For example, the facts are I am sick and weak, but the truth is the Lord is victorious in and through me. I kept reminding myself that the same power that created my body was living within to heal my body.

God's sense of humor was evident a few days later when I read in the Old Testament these words, "And the LORD said to Moses, Has the Lord's arm been shortened? Now you shall see whether what I say will happen to you or not."[156] Several weeks later while waiting for results from a bone scan, I was standing in my bathroom when I heard with my ears a voice say "No cancer in bones." Immediately my anxiety over those results disappeared. I spoke aloud, "God does want me well." That moment of His truth became my truth,[157] spurring me on to eat a little more and to cooperate with what He was doing inside me.

After months of crying out to the Lord for relief from pain, I finally tolerated a mild anxiety-relieving medication taken in minute doses. I was glad that all of the testing done showed nothing was seriously wrong with my body. I was appalled that I, as a Christian, had been downed by stress and tension from unresolved fears and conflicts.

In September a close friend, Celie Lewis, confided that she had started drinking carrot juice and barley green powder three times a day. Her strength and energy were improving. She wondered if I might want to think about doing this.

Deciding I had nothing to lose, I bought an inexpensive juicer, five pounds of carrots at a time, some barley green, powdered yeast, and began to experiment. My appetite improved over months of juicing carrots and fruits, and consuming fresh, raw vegetables. I have continued my juicing regimen, which has become an unplanned blessing for my eyes. In spite of aging, they have not deteriorated. My body still benefits from the chiropractor's skill.

As my emotions began to heal, my pain decreased in intensity. My fatigue and pain gradually faded over the next year as health returned, but learning how to constructively deal with stress and tension is an ongoing battle.

Another of Malachite's dark green bands of testing appeared several years later when throat problems returned. As my scarred throat area began narrowing, I knew months of labored breathing, weakness, anxiety, and discouragement. Finally, laser throat surgery increased my windpipe capacity for more normal (for me) breathing.

It seems the Lord jump-starts us by giving each of us a measure of faith, because "without faith it is impossible to please God."[158] Faith is His love gift to me: trust is my love gift to Him. Faith is believing not only what He has promised, but what He has finished in His realm, opening the door for it to happen in mine, as I trust Him to do it.

My Nurturer and Nourisher, El Shaddai, wanted to enrich me and increase my fruitfulness, but like Job, there were some things that needed changing inside first. Growing in His truth and light brought healing from stress, fears, and grief for the body of this unique Malachite stone.

SCRIPTURES and NOTES

149 1 Thessalonians 5:23

Now may the God of peace Himself sanctify you completely; and may your whole spirit, soul, and body be preserved blameless at the coming of our Lord Jesus Christ.

150 1 Samuel 9:3

Now the donkeys of Kish, Saul's father, were lost. And Kish said to his son Saul, Please take one of the servants with you, and arise, go look for the donkeys.

151 1 Samuel 9:20

But as for your donkeys that were lost three days ago, do not be anxious about them, for they have been found. And on whom is all the desire of Israel? Is it not on you and on all your father's house?

152 Matthew 10:39

153 Philippians 3:13

154 Job 3:25

155 Genesis 17:1

When Abram was ninety-nine years old, the Lord appeared to Abram and said to him, I am Almighty God (El Shaddai); walk before Me and be blameless.

156 Numbers 11:23

157 Jeremiah 30:17

For I will restore health to you and heal you of your wounds, says the Lord, because they called you an outcast saying: This is Zion; no one seeks her.

158 Hebrews 11:6

But without faith it is impossible to please Him, for he who comes to God must believe that He is, and that He is a rewarder of those who diligently seek Him.

BURGUNDY
The Color of Sanctification

Burgundy, the color of beets, is a deep, rich, intense combination of violet (red and blue) leaning toward the red. This shade serves as a bridge connecting the purple of one rainbow to the red of a second. Thus, Burgundy requires two parts of red to one of blue, the same way my soul needs two parts of love, (i.e., divine and human), added to His truth.

My spirit joined with the Lord's when I asked Him to be my Savior at nine years of age. My soul, another part of the inner me, likewise needs saving. In other words, my soul needs sanctifying.

To be sanctified is to be set apart by the Lord, to grow in holiness and consecration. The Lord included me when He prayed for all believers with these words, "Sanctify them by Your truth."[159] We are sanctified by the Lord of Love when we believe, and we are being sanctified as we grow in trust.

In the last chapter I mentioned dealing with the bodily aspects of my problems. In this one, my soul takes center stage. My soul, still smarting from wounds of grief, stress, and fears, needed cleansing and sanctifying. As mentioned before, the soul consists of three active parts, namely, the mind thinks, the will decides, and the emotions feel. In a healthy soul, these contribute equally, maintaining a wholesome balance.

Anguish throws the soul parts off balance. It is as debilitating as physical pain to the body. Death cripples the souls of those who are left to deal with the loss of loved ones. Emotions are raw, the mind is overwhelmed, and the will cannot function during grief, trauma, and stress.

With time, the sharp rawness of grief settled into a permanent dull ache inside. Fearful and sad, I was hurting in my soul where medicine is useless. I was disappointed and maybe resentful of the Lord's taking another loved one.

Emotionally I guess I was angry that I was sick, and impatient to recover. At least when I was well I could more easily avoid thoughts of death with its shroud of pain. The panic of never being well again set in. Yes, my emotions were running amok with no way to rein them in.

My dilemma was that if I trusted God as I had claimed, then physical death is part of that trust. I really tried to accept what was happening when I prayed,

> *Lord, I do not know how deaths fit in, but You do not make mistakes. I trust Your Sovereign right and timing so I release my brother and friend to Your perfect care.*

This should have solved the matter. However, I noticed that anytime eternity or heaven was mentioned, I still felt myself withdrawing, kind of like a turtle shrinking into his shell. Filled with unutterable sadness, I cried out to the Holy Spirit to help my soul grasp more of His truth, and received these words:

> Death is not the end, but the beginning of life in the spirit world where spirits, not bodies and souls, rule and reign.
>
> Sometimes release from earthly life is a very loving act I have performed, not just in the here and now, but down through the ages. I do not need disease, accidents, aging, violence or any other form of destruction to bring death to your physical bodies.
>
> I use the choices each of you makes to bring about My will on earth. The law of sowing and reaping is valid, operative, and usable. There are no accidents in My plans. Trust Me in the death of loved ones.

When I heard Him say the word "trust," I understood He was at work once again bringing to light my hidden fears and hurts.

However, not all that happened during these days was negative and painful. Because music has played a vital part in my well being since childhood, there was always a piano and/or organ in our home until after we moved to South Carolina. Then followed several instrument-less years before my husband solved his desire to have music in the home again by buying an inexpensive electronic keyboard.

I played it some, but it did not satisfy me. I guess every organist's favorite is a pipe organ. My second choice was the Hammond Organ with its enduring mechanism of tone wheels that could produce soft, soul-calming flute tones. Several of my organ teachers were Hammond experts and translated their love of the instrument to me.

Both of my married daughters and their families who live nearby knew I preferred the Hammond organ. What they did not know was my deep yearning to have one in my home again. They learned that a used Hammond spinet (like one I used to have) was going to be sold, and asked me if I were interested. Both of my daughters, music angels in disguise, made a trip to Atlanta and back on a rainy Saturday in July to bring me a beautiful Hammond organ in cherry wood finish. I was grateful for their safe trip. I was humbled by their caring. I was ecstatic about the organ.

Besides being able to enjoy all kinds of organ music once again, I worshipped through songs like "Rock of Ages," "Wonderful Peace," "Overshadowed," "Great Is Thy Faithfulness," "Clair de Lune," "Moonlight Sonata," and seasonal songs.

I do not know if music calms the savage beast, but it calmed my emotions so I could hear the Lord again. I confessed that I had felt like a failure deep inside (as if success determined worth). I confessed my lingering fear of death. I rested in Him and listened for His voice . . . .

> Through the music and words in your heart, I AM taking your fear of death, calming your soul, and giving you peace.
>
> Fear is an insidious foe. This is one of the fiery

darts Satan directs toward you. Fear was conquered by Me on the cross the same as sickness and other negative forces from the evil one.

Fear of disapproval and rejection, by Me and others, sneaks into the folds of everything you do. Fed by doubts and unbelief in My promises, you become stressed and anxious. Your fears of pain, weakness, premature dying, and confrontations are groundless.

You are in charge of your attitudes and choices. Love others, hear them gladly, then keep your own counsel. They are not in charge of your life; you and I are.

To be free to be the person I made you to be is what I want. Because you believe in Me, I have given you self-worth along with purpose. Accept it. Relax in it. Quit striving to have what is already a gift. As you grow stronger, you will be able to fight the good fight with My presence and power. I am lovingly preparing you. Trust Me.

My fixed income as a senior citizen was not keeping pace with inflation. Being frugal with my bare-bones budget was not enough. The only alternative was to increase my income. Just thinking about how I might do this produced anxiety and a hoarse throat.

The obvious option open to me was to start giving piano lessons again, but I did not want to. I took this to the Lord and prayed,

> *I am grateful for the training, experience, and ability to teach music. I have used it in the past to the fullest to help others be able to better serve Him, as well as to supplement our income. So far as I am concerned, this was all in the past, a closed chapter in my life.*

I also confessed that I felt guilty about teaching music when

I had not been able yet to return to teaching a Bible Study. I loved teaching God's Word to believers and was eager to do so again. I was sure teaching music would drain what time and energy I had away from my writing, my church, family, and friends.

One day at my computer, when I asked the Lord what I should do, I typed out this:

> I know all about your financial situation, and I AM already taking care of it. Trust me as your Provider, your Jehovah-Jireh,[160] in this. Your heart's desires coming to you from time to time are gifts from Me. Receive them as such.
>
> Everything that is happening to you is part of my plan for you, and it will all work together for good. You will see. Music is a vital part of your life and service, and will help complete you even now. That is why I gave You the organ. Your heart and emotions have been opened by your enjoyment of the organ tones and music. Pass this on. You are My choice to teach music to others.
>
> Besides fulfillment, you need the relating, the social give and take, and the added income. Do not fear what I have planned for you. Rest in Me. Trust Me. Use what you have for My honor and glory, whether it is writing, teaching, or ministering. You need not covet all your time for writing; spend it living each day to the fullest whatever the day holds. I love you, and I AM with you to bless you as you glorify Me.

This word from the Lord took away my fears, once again. He opened the doors for me to teach piano and keyboard. Before long I was enjoying lessons with many pupils of all ages. Because I had only the organ and a small keyboard in my home, I drove to their homes. It got me out of my home, and was fun to visit with families and their pets each week. Playing and teaching music are back as a vital part of my life, satisfying to my body, soul, and spirit.

One of our pastors at church, Jim Weathers, explained how playing the organ satisfies my body, soul, and spirit. Though performed physically with the body, it stimulates mental faculties and engages the emotions. However, spiritual refreshing overshadows my other benefits. Playing the organ resounds deeply inside because it touches my subconscious through beloved songs and hymns of my past. When my soul and spirit vibrate on the same frequency, healing results.

The Lord has taken the red of my budget, plus the red of grief-stress-fears, and infused both with His love. Next He blended them with the blue of His truth in music into a warm, rich burgundy for living. He has restored a healthy, wholesome balance of the mind, will, and emotions in my soul, thus sanctifying me for His use.

SCRIPTURES and NOTES

159 John 17:17

Sanctify them by Your truth. Your word is truth.

160 Genesis 22:14

And Abraham called the name of the place, The-Lord-Will-Provide; as it is said to this day, In the Mount of the Lord it shall be provided.

NAVY
The Color Of Righteousness

Navy is a dark, non-transparent shade of blue, appearing in the rainbow close to the midnight-blue-so-dark-it-looks-purple indigo. Navy is indicative of authority, in that it commands respect and a correct response. Blue is the spiritual color, thus it follows that navy represents both authority and integrity in my spirit.

Since navy blue communicates doing things right with authority, it pictures the righteousness of the Lord. Jeremiah wrote "This is the name by which He will be called: THE LORD OUR RIGHTEOUSNESS (JEHOVAH-TSIDKENU)."[161]

Human righteousness is very different from the Lord's righteousness because ours is clouded with sin and self. When we become believers, He covers us with His robe of righteousness.[162] God sees His Son's righteousness when He looks at us instead of the filthy rags of our righteousness.[163]

We cannot see through navy blue just like we cannot see through the things of the spirit. Paul wrote in the New Testament that "No one knows the things of God except the Spirit of God," and likewise no one "knows the things of a man except the spirit of the man."[164]

Since different words in the original Hebrew and Greek are used for spirit and soul, I believe both my spirit and soul are different entities with the capacity to grow; indeed, each does grow.

Whether spirit growth is leaping or infinitesimal, it is progress nonetheless. This progress can occur positively in growth toward the Lord, or negatively in growth away from Him toward darkness and evil.

The Lord's truth and light filled my fledgling spirit when I asked the Lord to be my Savior as a child. Because my spirit was joined with the Lord's, my re-created spirit bore the image of God, and could begin to take on the nature of God.

Spiritual growth through the years has allowed me to receive progressively more of Him.

I mentioned earlier that I would never forget my friend, Helen, who loaned our family her cabin for a week's vacation in July 1984 at Kentucky Lake. Each morning during that week I spent time alone with the Lord on the anchored pontoon. As I prayed and meditated, I watched, then wrote of the changes on the lake taking place before my eyes:

> Fog and mist fled before the light. . . as wickedness and darkness flee before Christ, the Light of the world. . . .
>
> Reflection is mine, and starts in my spirit. As the moon reflects the sun, I must reflect the Son. On a lake, the reflection of trees, flowers, and lights may be marred by waves, fish, frogs, bugs, currents, boats, and swimmers. In my life, the reflection of the Son may be marred by trouble, insecurities, crises, choices, and relationships.
>
> If my eyelids are lowered, I can see only the reflections which are distorted. That is the danger in depending on someone else's concept of God. We must each seek to know Him and His truths for ourselves.
>
> Reflection of water and waves is seen on trees and flowers. We cannot see inside of trees like we cannot see inside of Christ. Reflection on trees, caused by the perpetual motion of light reflected from water, is lovely to see. All committed believers reflect facets of His nature, but reflection is never as true as the source.
>
> Refraction differs in that it changes an image so it no longer mirrors the original. For example, a pencil in water looks bent below the water's surface. The water refracts the pencil's image. We humans refract the image of God by being descendants of Adam. At best, we can only give the world

> a distorted view of the Lord.
>
> I moved some from refracting to reflecting the Light of the world when I became a believer in Christ. However, my reflected image of the Lord is just a spark by which others ignite their own fires of knowing Him.

It seems that my spirit perceives the truth the Holy Spirit is giving long before I know how to assimilate it. For example, I believed the truth when I first read it that I was abiding "under the shadow of the Almighty."[165] Years later I began to see that abiding under the shadow of the Almighty was more than cowering under His wing. The Lord God Almighty was casting a tremendous, all-encompassing, loving shadow of protection and guidance over me. I had worth because God created me, saved me, and overshadowed me with His promise never to forsake me. When God's light shone on this verse, I received in my spirit the greater truth of who God was and what He was really saying.

I will never forget a prayer offered for me by Bill Stancil, one of the pastors in our church. Bill prayed:

> *Lord, pour Your healing power and presence into Shirley's spirit 'til it overflows, and runs down into her soul, where it ebbs and flows 'til it spills over into her body, bringing wholeness and health.*

I still pray that prayer because I believe the Lord intended for His wholeness and guidance to enter my spirit first, then pass over into my soul, and finally be seen in my body and actions. Sometimes I get this order all mixed up, as seen when I revert to former patterns and familiar reactions in times of crises and traumas. Bypassing my spirit's priority, I allow my emotions to control my body bringing on illness, severe pain, or disease. Pain drives me back to seek what God might have been saying or doing. Shame, embarrassment, and confession follow the realization that I have blown it again. The Lord forgives me, and we move on to the next stretching or testing time.

On occasion the Lord repeats my own words back to me, deep in my spirit. During a summer thunderstorm one night when my stress, fear, and grief were raging, a loud clap of thunder terrified my dog, Christy. As she whined, I reassured her with phrases like "I know it is thundering on you again, but it is okay. I'm right here with you."

Instantly I became aware of the Lord's presence, sitting right there beside me on my bed. He repeated,

> I know it is thundering on you again, but it is okay. I am right here with you. We will go through this painful time together. Faith is necessary to please Me, and trust follows as a knowing inside, an absolute assurance of truth and peace.
>
> To accept My love and grace when becoming a believer is overwhelming and awesome. My love, spreading out in eons of depth below this surface, is the greatest truth, and the strongest essential for all growth. That is why you must be strengthened with My Spirit in your spirit, and be rooted and grounded in the love of Christ, before you can be filled with the fullness of God.[166]
>
> You have a shortage of love. Let go of the old, dry shriveled love and hopes of love in your past that you keep trying to bring to life. You have been trying to receive Mine through the same pinched, weak way familiar to you. Instead of a weak trickle, open the flood gates of your spirit and soul, and let My abundance bless you and heal you. Read, ponder, surround yourself with verses of My love. Let My perfect love fill the empty hurt around your heart. I want you to relax in it, swim in it, float on it. Let Me carry you and satisfy all your longings.

When we humans design projects or renovations, we start measuring and working from the outside. The Lord works just the opposite and starts with the inside. The scriptures bear this out. In giving Moses the instructions for the tabernacle, He started in the Holy of Holies with specifics as to the Ark of the Covenant.[167]

He is still changing me from the inside out – spirit, soul, and body. Belonging to Christ and following Him has introduced changes in my spiritual stone shapes, stacking order, and mortar makeup. Change is painful, scary, and out of my control, but it is the only way He can "lead me in the paths of righteousness."[168] He is replacing my foggy fumbling with doing the right thing in the right way at the right time for the right reasons.

"God is a Spirit, and those who worship Him must worship in spirit and truth."[169] Spirit to spirit to Spirit. The truth, as authoritative as navy blue, is this: "For He (God) made Him (Christ) who knew no sin to be sin for us, that we might become the righteousness of God in Him."[170] Becoming the righteousness of God in Christ starts with our spirits calling for "THE LORD OUR RIGHTEOUSNESS (JEHOVAH-TSIDKENU)."[171] As the Lord imparts His righteousness to us, we "live for righteousness."[172]

SCRIPTURES and NOTES

161 Jeremiah 23:6

In His days Judah will be saved, and Israel will dwell safely; now this is His name by which He will be called: THE LORD OUR RIGHTEOUSNESS. (YHWH Tsidkenu)

162 Isaiah 61:10

I will greatly rejoice in the Lord, my soul shall be joyful in my God; for He has clothed me with the garments of salvation, He has covered me with the robe of righteousness, as a bridegroom decks himself with ornaments, and a bride adorns herself with her jewels.

163 Isaiah 64:6

But we are all like an unclean thing, and all our righteousnesses are like filthy rags; we all fade as a leaf, and our iniquities, like the wind, have taken us away.

164 1 Corinthians 2:11

165 Psalm 91:1

He who dwells in the secret place of the Most High shall abide under the shadow of the Almighty.

166 Ephesians 3:16-19

167 Exodus 25-31

168 Psalm 23:3

He restores my soul; He leads me in the paths of righteousness for His name's sake.

169 John 4:24

170 2 Corinthians 5:21

171 Jeremiah 23:6

In His days Judah will be saved, and Israel will dwell safely; now this is His name by which He will be called: THE LORD OUR RIGHTEOUSNESS. (YHWH Tsidkenu)

172 1 Peter 2:24

Who Himself bore our sins in His own body on the

tree, that we, having died to sins, might live for righteousness – by whose stripes you were healed.

GOLDEN HONEY
The Color of Victory

Clear red and yellow produce the light, lucid, irresistible color of golden honey that draws us like bees to flowers. This color remains transparent when more yellow is added, in much the same way that adding more light does not change the transparency of the love and light already at work in our growth.

As athletes in the Olympics aim for the gold, all of us aspire to bask in the golden glow of sweet victory. Through the years a banner or flag hoisted high has proclaimed the victor. We Americans proudly sing our national anthem born of when "Old Glory" was still flying over Fort McHenry in 1814 after a night of intense battle.

Moses named the altar of victory over the Amalekites, Jehovah-Nissi meaning "The-Lord-Is-My-Banner."[173] A banner can indicate love in addition to victory. King Solomon wrote, "His banner over me was love."[174] The banners of love and victory are offered freely since the Lord sacrificed Himself for us. King David said the Lord desires to satisfy us with honey from the rock[175] meaning the sweetness of love and victory are ours through the Rock Himself. When He returns as victorious King, we "win the gold" by walking in His golden light on streets of gold, clear as honey.

In the meantime, trust remains an opportunity for growth in some area and always comes with a price tag. It costs me the continual releasing of the control of my life. Trust engages body, soul, spirit, conscious, subconscious, and unconscious. These are so inextricably woven that a loose thread in one area disturbs the effectiveness of the others. My being imperfect guarantees that I have loose threads in all areas!

The Holy Spirit is continually enlightening, repairing, and replacing brokenness. However, growth is never automatic. The catalyst for body growth is food; for soul growth is change; for spiritual peace is unrest. Change and unrest drive us to trust.

Trust is earned, not given. God earned our trust before He created anything by providing for us from before the foundation of the world. Pollen is free to the bees like faith is a free gift. God gives each of us a measure of faith that we take, use, and return to Him as trust in that area. When we use faith, we get a honey of a trust.

Trust demands a decision by us, a commitment beyond the call of faith. It is hard to trust people because they fail us. It is maybe harder to trust the Lord whom we cannot see, but it is vitally important to Him and us.

This chapter deals with my trust level in the present, and how the Lord is still stretching me toward wholeness. For example, in June of 2000 lightning destroyed the modem on my computer. In addition to my pain and weakness that year, this seemed like the last straw. I felt like Job must have, but like Job I decided to trust God through it all. I was excited when I learned that my home insurance covered lightning damage, and ecstatic when I became the owner of a new iMac in a gorgeous aquamarine color. I could see that the Lord really was working all things together for good, in spite of my loss.

With a grateful heart, I thanked Him and prayed,

> "Holy Spirit, keep reminding me that problems are opportunities for You to work, and for me to be stretched into new growth."

The Lord responded with:

> Trust is always hard because it is built on faith and hope, not of tangible materials. I love you and I AM with you all the way, through the pain, the testing, and the overcoming. I will not fail you now or ever. Place your eggs of relinquishment, one by one, into My basket called "Trust," for I AM trustworthy.

The God of creativity had given me a new approach! Into His Basket of Trust I decided to place the first egg – my nerves.

The second was pain. The third egg to let go of was grieving. I knew the Lord was walking with me through the molasses of grief, but I needed to place my emotional losses and hurts into His basket of trust. Another egg I released was my past. My security was not found in the family, friends, places, or events of my past, but in Him alone.

Holding the fear-of-death egg in my hand above His basket, I remembered that a caterpillar's darkest hour is the brightest for the butterfly. To die is to be instantly changed into a spirit being which remains a mystery to us. The Lord gave us humans a strong will to survive, so it is natural to cling to life. But an unhealthy fear of death changes the equation, and adds stress. When dying grace is needed, the Lord will provide it. I need not carry around the "dread-of-not-living egg" anymore, so I set it in the "Trust Basket" where it belonged, along with the others.

Since all of these eggs are out of my control, I released them to the "Basket Holder." These specific eggs are definites, not generalities. They break up my problems into workable solutions, each containing the germ of life and food for growth. Because the raw eggs of my hidden thoughts and motives are easily broken and messy, I need His light to keep on shining into the recesses of my being.

When I am faced with a new problem, I do not know at the outset whether it is a time of new growth, or a time of testing to check out past growth. Either way, the crisis is real, and trust is at stake once again – no matter what, as seen in the following story.

Arriving at the local veterinary clinic on a Friday morning, I apprehensively opened the door and tugged on the leash of Christy, my toy fox terrier, who was reluctant to enter. For a week I had put peroxide and Panolog ointment on the protruding sore on my dog's neck below her left jaw as Dr. Mackinnon had suggested. Today he would tell me whether it was an infected bite or cyst.

After examining her, he said, "It is an infected cyst that

should be removed as soon as possible." I nodded in agreement. But then he added, "Of course, we will send it away to be tested."

Tested? I had not thought beyond a cyst. . . beyond surgery to remove it. Now my thoughts ran rampant. I held myself together until Christy and I were back in the car. Then "what ifs" took over, causing tears to cloud my vision. *"What if she's got cancer?" . . . "How do they treat cancer in pets?" . . . "What if I have to put her to sleep?" . . . "I know pets do not last forever, but what if I lose her . . ."*

Christy was glad to be back in the car with me, and she settled down for a nap on the way home, blissfully unaware of impending events. Glancing at her I thought, *I have loved fox terriers all my life, ever since my parents gave me one for my first birthday. I know Christy is just a dog, but she is more than that to me. She is my friend, and has been my canine companion for five years now. Because my husband got her for me three months before he was killed in an accident, she is all the more special to me.*

I talk to her about everything as if she comprehends it all. Most of the time she just stands there and listens with her head cocked slightly to the side as if she is thinking about what I am saying. Other times our conversations are two-way, as she responds with sort-of-half-way-whines or growl-sounds that may last about the length of a sentence, or longer. She knows my habits and daily routine so well that when I get off schedule, she comes where I am, sits and whines. Christy is not the cuddly type of small lap dog. She weighs in at 15 pounds and prefers to stand in my lap, leaning against me, which prompted my family to dub her "Christy Ilean."

She is easy to bathe for she jumps into the bathtub, and likes to be dried with the hair dryer. Christy sleeps on my bed at night under a baby-sized thermal blanket. She spends her days on the twin bed in the guest room looking out the window to see what is passing by. She recognizes my daughters' cars a half a block away (even when I have not told her they are coming). Golf carts and cats are on her hate list. When either one appears she starts barking, then races down the hall, through the kitchen, and out her pet door at 80 miles an hour. She continues barking furiously from the fenced-in yard 'til the adversary is gone. She never touches anything not hers, but plays with her own toys. She is an almost perfect dog . . . and I could not imagine being without her.

Arriving home after our visit to the vet, I did mundane chores that left my mind to run amok, causing havoc with my nerves and feelings. Christy responded to my crying by looking up into my face until I let her jump onto my lap. She comforted me by laying her head on my shoulder, then trying to lick my face. Just being able to put both of my arms around her and hold her warm body was comforting. I held her and told her (for the millionth time) that I loved her and I needed her.

Heather, my daughter, called Friday afternoon and found me not coping well at all with the possible loss of Christy. She said, "Pack your bags. You do not need to be alone this weekend, so I am coming to get you and Christy now." Her family, living not far from the beach, had a shar-pei dog named Simba and a de-clawed cat called Oreo. We went with her – right into an incredible weekend filled with love and hugs, good food, laughter at mishaps, and misty eyes as we talked.

Christy and Simba related as friends, romping and chasing and sleeping in the sun. Oreo remained Enemy Number One to my dog. Heather had to keep the cat fastened when Christy was free, and vice versa. Friday evening when Oreo went upstairs, I took Christy's leash off allowing her to sniff around the first floor including the master bedroom. The cat came back downstairs, was caught, put in the bedroom, and the door was closed leaving them inadvertently together in the dark. Oblivious to it all, we sat around talking in the living room, 'til a frenzied ruckus of barks and meows shattered the moment. Heather opened the door, Christy came running out, and Oreo was on the bed with all her fur standing up. We calmed the animals. Then the more we thought about it, the funnier it got, and we dissolved in laughter at our stupidity. The very thing we had tried so hard to avert was the very thing we had caused!

Like a dry sponge, I soaked up precious moments of sharing privately with each one. When Heather and I talked, our conversation moved from the love of pets to the deeper waters of how she and I personally give and receive love, even to each other.

We agreed that the need for immediate, loving responses in traumas or crises are as important to our bodies and souls as the long term gains of medicine and counseling. By contrast, rejection (real or imagined) leads to pain and disease within. We faced the fact that in spite of our busy lives, it was not good to put off spending time together, talking, and loving – that precious, necessary thing that families can do for each other. I returned home with Christy late Sunday afternoon better able to deal with the difficult week ahead.

I prayed, reminding the Lord about such things as:

> *I know You care about all that You have created, for Your word says "You feed the sparrows"*[176] *and "not one of them falls to the ground without the Father's notice."*[177]
>
> *I do not find anywhere in the Bible where You healed animals, but You said, "My Father in heaven will give good things to those who ask Him."*[178] *So I am asking You to heal Christy totally, not because Christy or I either one deserve it, but because You love me.*
>
> *I know You created Christy and gave her to me, but, Lord, she is in trouble. This cyst-growth-tumor on her neck scares me because I may lose her. That makes it harder for me to release Christy to You, but nevertheless I am choosing to let go and to trust You no matter what . . .*

Tuesday, the day of surgery arrived. I took Christy early to the vet's office where she would be all day. The receptionist at the clinic called me in the afternoon to say there were no complications during her procedure and she was slowly waking up. About 5 p.m. I brought her home with four staples holding her wound together, gave her water, fed her a small amount, and pampered her with doggie treats.

The days dragged by - Wednesday - Thursday - Friday - Saturday - days of her healing, and my waiting for her test results, - days during which my thoughts and prayers raced like horses wanting to reach the finish line. *How much longer must I wait? Was she hurting from the staples? Sore from the surgery? I wish the vet would ring. Lord, I'm still trusting she will be okay.* I recalled how three years earlier Christy was my 24/7 companion during my recovery from major surgery; now it was my turn to take care of her. *Come on, phone, ring! And let it be the vet this time.*

Saturday about noon the phone rang. Anxiously answering it (as I did each time it rang), I heard the receptionist at the clinic say, "Christy's test results just came in, and her tumor is benign." My breath caught in my throat. A huge smile appeared, as I sent a *"Thank You"* heavenward. Relieved! Thrilled! Ecstatic! Midst joyful weeping I managed to choke out a thank you to her for calling so soon. I immediately told Christy who licked my wet face and did not understand what all the fuss was about.

The Lord's "yes" answer to my prayers for her does not determine my trust in Him, anymore than a "no" answer would have negated it. Because the Lord and I had endured a lifetime of experiences together, I had begun to grasp at last how highly He values "trust." I knew God loves me and cares about the things that concern me. But by healing Christy, He ministered to my needs as well as hers. My heart overflows with gratitude to the Lord for my family, and for His goodness to my pet and me. Through this experience, I learned a little more about trusting Him with everything, no matter what.

As you can see, trusting the Lord completely is still a work in progress. I can choose to agree with God's Word about everything, everyday – or not. But, choosing His way means I must give up my own. I am learning that wholeness is not a one-time deal, but a reality that comes at different times and on different levels, determined by my choices. Choosing to trust Him in everything enlightens my path, and assures me of victory as sweet and wholesome as golden honey.

SCRIPTURES and NOTES

173 Exodus 17:15

And Moses built an altar and called its name, The-Lord-Is-My-Banner (Jehovah Nissi).

174 Song of Solomon 2:4

He brought me to the banqueting house, and his banner over me was love.

175 Psalm 81:16

He would have fed them also with the finest of wheat; and with honey from the rock I would have satisfied you.

176 Matthew 6:26

Look at the birds of the air, for they neither sow nor reap nor gather into barns: yet your heavenly Father feeds them. Are you not of more value than they?

177 Matthew 10:29

Are not two sparrows sold for a copper coin? And not one of them falls to the ground apart from your Father's will.

178 Matthew 7:11

If you then, being evil, know how to give good gifts to your children, how much more will your Father who is in heaven give good things to those who ask Him!

FUCHSIA
The Color Of Hope

Fuchsia shouts its essence of bright, purplish red. Adding more red to a purplish blend produces this magenta color. Its intensity magnetizes us, grabs our attention. When the King of Kings (in the purple of royalty) adds His abundance of love (red), the fuchsia of hope emerges. And hope always paints a rosy future.

When Isaiah wrote, "I saw the Lord sitting on a throne, high and lifted up,"[179] he was seeing Him as King, and used the Hebrew word Adonai meaning "the Lord reigns." The Lord Jesus Christ is called the King of Kings three times in the New Testament, further establishing His identity for us. He is to be worshipped and is worthy of our adoration.

I began to worship the Lord Jesus Christ as "King of Kings" years ago, but have spent a lifetime learning how to worship Him as "Lord of Lords." Nothing happens by accident, nor is it an event unto itself. Everything is caused – a sowing and reaping process – whereby growth comes. Growing in trust is more than just knowing about Him. It is the alive awareness of the Lord's presence, power, and caring in everything that happens. His thoughts toward us are of peace, hope, and a future.[180] The rosy glow of hope abides deep within.

When we romantics think of falling in love and marrying, we dream of finding the perfect mate. When that vision of perfection comes our way, we can hardly wait to marry. But, alas, the vision grows blurry over time, until at last it only shimmers as a mirage on the horizon of our dreams. The imperfections of human lovers clash as we fight for control, or try to accept the unchangeable. But, when we fall in love with the Lord, our dreams of being loved perfectly come true.

A divine-human partnership is an amazing process. Someone has said, "Without God, we can not; without us He will not." It is almost unfathomable that the Lord God Almighty has limited Himself in order to partner with us. What we each contribute is beautifully expressed by the following quote:

God provides the colors; we paint the pictures.
God provides the notes; we write the music.
God provides the soil; we plant the flowers.
God provides the mind; we do the thinking.
God provides the gifts; we do the ministry.

I would add, "God provides the experiences; we do the trusting." Trust is more than believing; it is active obedience.

Beyond all our believing and doing is the truth that the Lord is growing us from "self" toward Him. I like Watchman Nee's description of Christian growth in loving God as found in the Old Testament book, "The Song of Songs."[181] We believers all start out by thinking of "ME" only, but over time it becomes "ME and God." With more experiences we move to "ME and GOD," then on to "GOD and me."

The first seven chapters in this book covered the basic things I knew about God, bringing me through the stages to "ME and GOD." The new things I learned about the Lord are seen in chapters 9-24. Over these years my love for Him increased bringing me through the fourth level of growth, i.e. "GOD and me." My spiritual goal now is to progress to the place where it is just "GOD" every time. To choose God's will and way first is the ultimate level of trust. Only then can I say, "He is Lord of Lords to me." A fuchsia future and hope await those who can trust the Lord "in everything, (and) give thanks; for this is the will of God in Christ Jesus for you."[182]

SCRIPTURES and NOTES

179 Isaiah 6:1

In the year that King Uzziah died, I saw the Lord sitting on a throne, high and lifted up, and the train of His robe filled the temple.

180 Jeremiah 29:11

For I know the thoughts that I think toward you, says the Lord, thoughts of peace and not of evil, to give you a future and a hope.

181 Watchman Nee, THE SONG OF SONGS, (Fort Washington, Pennsylvania: Christian Literature Crusade, 1965)

182 I Thessalonians 5:18

RAINBOW

GROWTH

MY RAINBOW GROWTH

The Color of Purpose

Writing about what the Lord has shown me and done for me is the source of my writing, so far. The Lord had a larger purpose beyond the solutions for what I have experienced. This purpose, I believe, is to let others know that "with God all things are possible."[183]

Writing seems to have been on the back burner most of my life. I did serve on the staff of my high school newspaper, The Record, and as a senior attended a conference in Lexington, Kentucky for journalists. Fast forward about 10 years when I looked at the bound copy of my thesis for the first time, and saw my name on the spine and front cover. I remember thinking *I would like to write a real book and see my name listed as the author.*

Other than writing my prayers and thoughts regularly, the dream of writing lay dormant for about 20 years. Then I began by entering short story contests, never winning. I rewrote, and resubmitted, and received rejections regularly for the next 14 years. Finally, after about 46 rewrites, Guideposts bought the story of my "trach" experience with the two-year-old girl in my hospital room.

My stories have been woven on the loom of trusting God; the warp is God's part, the weft (woof) is mine. His input started the shuttle flying, as seen here:

> Shirley, write your book to Me and for Me and by Me. After all it is about us and what we have been doing together through the years. I (Jesus) pleased the Father with telling of our past and doing what pleased Him. Follow me. You write it down, and I will do the rest.

I responded with,

> *Here am I, Lord, with pen in hand and computer*

keys at my fingertips to be Yours in our joint creative process.

After a time when my loom grew silent, He prodded me on:

> I cannot take you farther in learning to trust until you are doing what I called you to do. Your blank pages are creating blocks to your growth. You are My tongue and My pen.
>
> I planted inside you the desire and gift for writing to be used as the answer to your heart's cry to count for Me. Just as I commanded those in the Bible to write My words, I AM commanding you to write about Me, what I have done for you, and Who I AM to you.
>
> This writing entails your learning to trust, but it is really about Me and My ways. Trust indicates growth, the way a gauge indicates poundage or water level. Higher numbers mean greater pressure. In each experience you move from milk to meat, from faith to trust, thus bumping your trust up a notch. Growth, as I planned it, decreases stress though pressure builds.
>
> I AM with you, so take off your brakes and move into high gear with writing the books and stories I am leading you to do. I AM in charge, orchestrating it all. BUT my hands are tied 'til you get it on paper!
>
> Dream about your book; move it to a front burner and add the ingredients I bring to your mind to improve the flavor. I will be with you to guide you each step of the way. I have restored your health and energy, provided for you financially, and blessed you with family and friends so you are free to write and complete what we have started.
>
> "To everything there is a season, a time for every purpose under heaven."[184] This is your time to

write. "It is to your advantage not only to be doing what you began, but now you must complete it."[185]

This book is our priority. It does not mean you get uptight about it or so scheduled that you have no time for anything or anyone else. Helping others is important, but our priority is to capture in words what I have taught you. Become pregnant with it. Your delivery date will be your deadline for completing it.

Use your time wisely. Redeem it daily by doing what I have called and prepared you to do. Remember, I AM able, so trust Me to complete that which I have started in you.[186]

The unique way each one of us travels on the road of life has been expressed by this quote:

Our lives are but fine weavings,
That God and we prepare,
Each life becomes a fabric planned,
And fashioned in His care,

We may not always see just how
The weavings intertwine,
But we must trust the master's hand,
And follow His design,

For He can view the pattern
Upon the upper side,
While we must look from underneath
And trust in Him to guide.

Sometimes a strand of sorrow
Is added to His plan,
And though it's difficult for us,
We still must understand,

That it's He who fills the shuttle,

It's He who knows what's best,
So we must weave in patience,
And leave to Him the rest.
Not till the loom is silent,
And the shuttles cease to fly,
Shall God unroll the canvas,
And explain the reason why –

The dark threads are as needed,
In the weaver's skillful hand,
As the threads of gold and silver,
In the pattern He has planned.[187]

As you can see my weaving process is not finished, nor have the added shades of color been completed. The seven basic colors of the rainbow have expressed to me seven basic facets of the Lord, i.e. Love, Forgiveness, Light, Power, Truth, Holiness, and Kingship. The added shades, placed strategically between the colors, point to the newer experiences, hard times, and painful hours during which the Lord taught me something new about Himself, such as His Faithfulness, Goodness, and Changelessness.

He called me to write of Him, for Him, and about what He has done. He reigns as the Righteous King and Victorious Lord. I am still learning how to trust Him as my Shepherd, Healer, Helper, Peace, Provider, Comforter, Sanctifier and Rock. Now He has asked me to trust Him to complete that which He has started in me. As long as I live, He will be teaching me new things about Himself, resulting in more rainbow growth.

When I found myself getting uptight as I was preparing the query letters, book proposal, and CDs of my manuscript for the publishing process, I prayed, *"Lord, would You give me a picture and verses to help me trust You more through this preparation time?"*

I saw myself lying on a surfboard, holding on

for dear life. When I realized the Lord, pictured as light, was beside me, and how ridiculous I looked struggling to hang onto the surfboard as if it all depended on me, I laughed out loud.

Next I understood that the Lord is also my surfboard through these turbulent, awaited waves. I can lie down, sit up, or stand as we navigate the publishing waters. I can go fearfully or victoriously as I ride the creaming, curling waves or cruise through the wave troughs. He wants me to lean my whole weight on Him, to trust Him for He knows the pathways through the sea.

"Thus says the Lord, who makes a way in the sea and a path through the mighty waters,[188] 'Fear not, for I am with you; be not dismayed, for I am your God. I will strengthen you, yes, I will help you.'"[189]

In the basic rainbow, you cannot tell where one color stops and another starts. The same is true with the facets of God, such a love, peace, forgiveness and grace. It is a blending; a flowing, not separate entities. If you want red, you get all the colors. If you want love, you get all the facets of the Trinity. In one of the languages of central Europe, the rainbow is called "the bridge of the Holy Spirit."[190]

The rainbow arches across the sky right into our hearts. Each color curves with beauty, promise, and growth. Because the Lord has continued to use the rainbow to convey His truths to me personally, I hope and pray that your spanning these colors of trust with me has spurred you on toward maturity in Him.

SCRIPTURES and NOTES

183 Luke 1:37

For with God nothing will be impossible.

184 Ecclesiastes 3:1

185 2 Corinthians 8:10-11

It is to your advantage not only to be doing what you began and were desiring to do a year ago, but now you also must complete the doing of it: that as there was a readiness to desire it, so there also may be a completion out of what you have.

186 Philippians 1:6

Being confident of this very thing, that He who has begun a good work in you will complete it until the day of Jesus Christ.

187 Author unknown, "The Plan of the Master Weaver."

188 Isaiah 43:16

189 Isaiah 41:10

Fear not, for I am with you; be not dismayed, for I am your God. I will strengthen you, yes, I will help you; I will uphold you with my righteous right hand.

190 Walter J. Saucier, WORLD BOOK, Vol 16, Field Enterprises Educational Corporation, 1974, p 127.

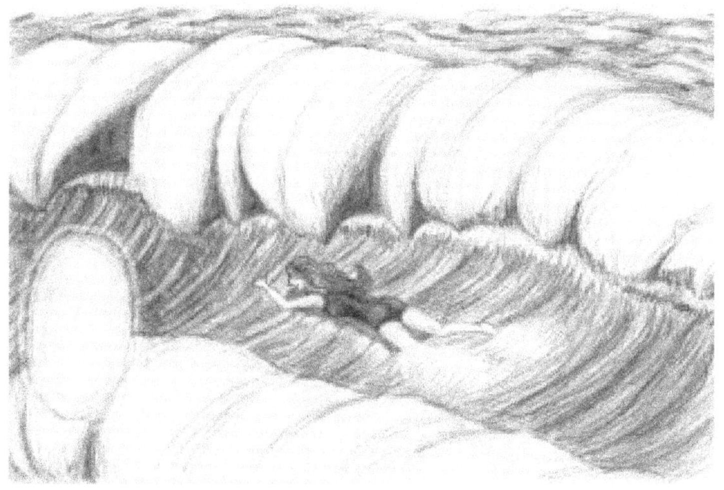

SURFING

Because I was getting uptight as I was getting ready for the publishing process, I prayed, *"Lord, would You give me a picture and verses to help me trust You more through this preparation time?"*

I saw myself lying on a surfboard, holding on for dear life. When I realized the Lord, pictured as light, was beside me, and how ridiculous I looked struggling to hang onto the surfboard as if it all depended on me, I laughed out loud.

Next I understood that the Lord is also my surfboard through these turbulent, awaited waves. I can lie down, sit up, or stand as we navigate the publishing waters. I can go fearfully or victoriously as I ride the creaming, curling waves or cruise through the wave troughs. He wants me to lean my whole weight on Him, to trust Him for He knows the pathways through the sea.

"Thus says the Lord, who makes a way in the sea and a path through the mighty waters, "Fear not, for I am with you; be not dismayed, for I am your God. I will strengthen you, yes, I will help you."

THE ROSE

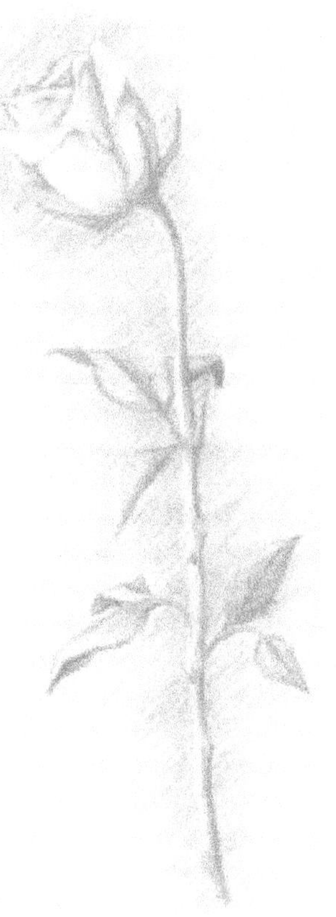

It is only a tiny rosebud -
    A flower of God's design;
But I cannot unfold the petals
    With these clumsy hands of mine.

The secret of unfolding flowers
    Is not known to such as I -
The flower God opens so sweetly
    In my hands would fade and die.

If I cannot unfold a rosebud
    This flower of God's design,
Then how can I think I have wisdom
    To unfold this life of mine?

So I'll trust in Him for His leading
    Each moment of every day,
And I'll look to Him for His guidance
    Each step of the pilgrim way.

For the pathway that lies before me
    My heavenly Father knows -
I'll trust Him to unfold the moments
    Just as He unfolds the rose.[191]

SCRIPTURES and NOTES

191 Author unknown, “The Rosebud.”

BIBLIOGRAPHY

BOOKS

Kuhlman, Kathryn. GOD CAN DO IT AGAIN, (Englewood Cliffs, New Jersey: Prentice-Hall, Inc., Guideposts Edition), 1969.

Morgan, David. ICONS OF AMERICAN PROTESTANTISM: THE ART OF WARNER SALLMAN, (New Haven:Yale University Press, 1966), p 65-66.

Marshall, Catherine. A MAN CALLED PETER, (New York: McGraw-Hill, 1951), p 59.

Maus, Cynthia Pearl. CHRIST AND THE FINE ARTS: AN ANTHOLOGY OF PICTURES, POETRY, MUSIC, AND STORIES CENTERING IN THE LIFE OF CHRIST. (New York: Harper & Brothers, 1959, p 539-541.

Nee, Watchman. SONG OF SONGS, (Fort Washington, Pennsylvania: Christian Literature Crusade, 1965), p. 94, 139.

Roberts, Oral. THE MIRACLE BOOK, (Tulsa, Oklahoma: Pinoak Publications), 1972.

Sanford, Agnes Mary White. THE HEALING LIGHT, (New York, New York: Ballantine Publishing Group), revised 1972.

Saucier, Walter J. WORLD BOOK, Vol 16, Field Enterprises Educational Corporation, 1974, p 127.

Siegel, Dr. Bernie. LOVE, MEDICINE & MIRACLES, (New York: Perennial Library, Harper & Row Publishers, 1986), p 74.

Stapleton, Jean Carter. THE GIFT OF INNER HEALING, (Waco, Texas: Word Publishing Co.), 1976.

MAGAZINE

Guideposts Associates, "GUIDEPOSTS," (Carmel, New York: Guideposts Associates, Inc.).

POEMS

Author unknown, "The Plan of the Master Weaver."

Author unknown, "The Rosebud."

SONG

Faber, Frederick W. "There's a Wideness in God's Mercy," 1862.

INDEX

About the Author

Shirley Bard was born in 1932 to a Christian family who fostered her acceptance of the Lord and gave her a foundation of spiritual strength. She publicly expressed her faith and was baptized at age nine, but as childhood illnesses led to multiple throat surgeries and the possibility that she might never be able to speak again, Shirley struggled to understand and to develop her relationship with God. Through some extraordinary visions and a lifelong commitment to seeking Him, she learned to see the rainbow as the ultimate sign of God's promises, and today, she invites others to explore the variants of the rainbow colors as they reach deeper levels of trust.

Many of Shirley's life experiences as a teen, a teacher, a pastor's wife, a mother, a grandmother – and now, a widow – parallel those shared by countless other Christians of all ages and levels of spiritual maturity. Her readers and friends not only relate to her quest for God's peace during trials, but also apply her stories to the challenges of everyday life.

Now living in Charleston, South Carolina, Shirley is a freelance writer whose inspirational stories have been published in well-known periodicals such as "Guideposts" and "Home Life."

Shirley holds a masters degree in education from the University of Louisville. She received her undergraduate degree from Georgetown College in Kentucky where she majored in education and minored in music. When she is not writing, spending time with family, or teaching piano lessons in the North Charleston area, she enjoys reading with her Kindle 3 and playing with her Chihuahua-Terrier mix, Honey-Girl. She is an avid reader who prefers being inspired, entertained, and challenged by Christian writing.